Teacher expectations and pupil learning

Roy Nash
Director, Rural Education Research Unit
University College of North Wales

Routledge & Kegan Paul
London, Henley and Boston

First published in 1976
by Routledge & Kegan Paul Ltd
39 Store Street,
London WC1E 7DD,
Broadway House,
Newtown Road,
Henley-on-Thames,
Oxon RG9 1EN and
9 Park Street,
Boston, Mass. 02108, USA
Manuscript typed by Muriel Edwards
Printed and bound in Great Britain by
Redwood Burn Limited
Trowbridge & Esher
© Roy Nash 1976

ISBN 0 7100 8338 6

Teacher expectations and pupil learning

Contents

Contents

Acknowledgments

The original suggestion that I should write this book for the Students Library of Education series was made by Professor Brian Simon. The task of reading the first drafts went to Professor J. R. Webster and to my colleagues in the Rural Education Research Unit, Dr Howard Williams and Marisse Evans. My greatest debt is certainly to Professor Ben Morris who, as editor, cleared up many obscure passages and helped me to correct several errors of interpretation. All have my sincere thanks.

Acknowledgements

Introduction

The present work will discuss those studies which have
tried to get to grips with the inter-related opinions,
attitudes, feelings and actions of teachers and pupils
in the classroom. It will look at the perceptions
teachers and pupils have of each other, the impact of
classroom organisation on patterns of interaction, the
effect of teachers' 'expectations' on pupils' performance
and so on.

There are people who have always appreciated that
teaching is not just a matter of filling empty heads with
facts. They have understood that teaching is vitally
concerned with personal relationships. Relationships
between teachers and teachers, teachers and pupils, and
pupils and pupils. But one group who have seemed slow to
grasp this, until quite recently anyway, are educational
researchers. Over the years they have developed a whole
series of standardised tests of ability and intelligence,
accumulated a vast quantity of data on demographic variables (social class, family size, school type and so on)
and established the correlations of success and failure
within the school system in these terms. No one wants
to suggest that the achievements of all this research
have not been worthwhile, but it has certainly distracted
attention from the workface of education – the classroom.
In the typical classroom – one may almost say in every
classroom – there is a teacher and a number of pupils.
The teacher is adult, in charge, and trained to instruct
her pupils in a number of valued skills. The pupils are
children, under authority, and directed to learn whatever
they are given. After only a little exposure to main-
stream educational research one might imagine that the
teacher and the pupils were mere puppets acting out, as
if without will or consciousness, performances directed
by the push and pull of outside forces. Sociologists

and psychologists probably don't intend their work to
leave this impression but they generally manage it all
the same. Butcher's (1968) regularly revised and
influential survey of educational research in Britain
illustrates the emphases of this tradition perfectly.
Not one study related to perceptions and attitudes is
mentioned throughout.

It might be helpful to mention some of the general
characteristics of the type of research we are concerned
with. Except for the most empirical work most studies
derive from what, in some circles, is called 'grand'
theory. Freudian theory, Gestaltist field theory and
symbolic interaction, to mention the three most important,
have been significant influences on educational research
in this area. It is because he works within a particular
theoretical orientation that the researcher formulates
the hypotheses he does. In order to test hypotheses the
researcher's concepts must be operationalised - that is
translated into measures. This is the crucial methodological problem. Suppose, for the sake of example, that
a researcher wants to test the hypothesis that self-
concept is related to school achievement. The former
will present no problem, there are dozens of acceptable
ability tests, but it will probably be necessary to
design a way of testing self-concept. Almost certainly
the researcher will construct a paper and pencil test, a
kind of questionnaire, in fact. It might include such
items as, 'I'm good at school', 'I'm OK at most things'
and 'I'm proud of the marks I get in class.' The
theoretical definitions of self-concept which led to the
original hypothesis will have been highly abstract but
the operational definition will be concrete and simple.
Sometimes, though not very often, the researcher will
make sure that all the test items are correlated with
each other. This provides at least some assurance that
all the items are measuring the same basic idea. It is
assumed on commonsense grounds that the measures will
have some relationship to the theoretical concept the
researcher started out with. There is no way of making
sure that it does: it must be assumed. Well over half of
the studies described in this book use a paper and pencil
test of some sort to provide operational definitions of
theoretically defined concepts.

It commonly happens that different concepts derived
from different theories have in practice very similar
operational definitions. The questions above were given
as examples of a test of self-concept. Imagine now a
researcher whose interest is not in self-concept but in
attitudes. Among the items included in his test are 'I

get on well in school', 'I like the lessons I have' and
'School is OK for me really.' These items measure attitude to school and the former set measure self-concept.
The concepts may be dissimilar but once operationalised
there is a close resemblance. The similarity of the items
will be unintended and easily overlooked. The conclusions
given in research journals - and there is a strong temptation to read only the conclusions, summaries or abst-
racts - will state that a correlation has been observed
between self-concept and ability or attitudes to school
and ability, as the case may be, and only in the main
body of the article, probably in small print, will it be
revealed that the tests used to measure both concepts have
more than a little in common.

That so many concepts derive from different theories
makes for another problem. There has to be a respect for
serious attempts to conceptualise experience scientific-
ally. It is only through the development of precisely
defined concepts that a science can progress. Yet there
is a difference between the language of science and the
jargon of technical terms. There is no real excuse, for
example, for the word 'subjects' (or even worse 'Ss')
where children or teachers are meant. Writing about social science research in ordinary language is more difficult than it seems. There is a long tradition of doing
just the opposite and it can be unnerving suddenly to
realise that stripped of jargon what one wanted to say
sounds much less impressive.

It is difficult to see how the worth of a study can be
appreciated unless the theoretical background and the
methodological procedures are known. Consequently I have
made a point of giving the fullest details about the
research discussed here. Details of the studies - time,
place, numbers, instruments, relationship to previous
work - all are essential to any reasoned criticism. Too
often we are given only the conclusions of a study, for
example, 'Smith (1970) showed that self-concept was
related to strong parental discipline.' Only if we are
able to look up the original study will we learn that
Smith used as a measure of self-concept a list of such
items as, 'I am generally pleased with the things I do -
Yes/No/Don't know' and as a measure of parental discipline
ratings by the children's teachers. And that these measures were found to be correlated in a sample of 36 secondary school pupils. Knowing this it is possible to examine
the findings critically. Without this information there
is no chance of doing so. There is only one way to understand research and that is to read it raw. It can be
tedious, mistaken, wrong-headed and it can also be intell-

igent, thought-provoking and ingenious. For those of us
who get hooked it is the only thing there is. But I know
that it is unreasonable to expect students who read this
book to look up more than a few of the studies it reports.
In any case a lot of the material is not easily available.
A good college library will take the major British journals but it is unlikely to have more than a few of the
American journals, if any, and ordinary students do not
normally have access to the inter-library loan system. It
is for this reason also that I have included as many details as possible: the critical student should have enough
to work on.

One last point. It may seem that there is a disjunc-
tion between the first chapter and those that follow. A
conviction is growing among many of us that research must
be interpreted within an overall theory of social action.
The interactionist theory outlined in the next few pages
is intended to provide an over-arching theory which can
be seen to relate together the empirical studies which
follow. It is not essential and readers who do not find
the argument useful or convincing are free to skip it.

Chapter one

Some theoretical considerations

I hope this chapter will be a little easier to read than
it was to write. Its aim is simple enough: I want to
bring some conceptual clarity to the findings of recent
research concerned with the actions of teachers and
pupils. The difficulty stems from the multitude of
concepts used by various writers in this field. One will
use the term 'expectations' where another will use
'norms'. Again, one will use the word 'opinion' as syn-
onymous with 'attitude' where another will make a clear
distinction, which has importance for his own work,
between the two terms. One solution to this problem of
terminology might be to define precisely in advance all
the concepts which will appear in the pages to follow.
This might make for clarity but it would also make for
tedious reading. Instead, each concept will be defined
as it is introduced and where my definition differs
significantly from that of other writers these differences will be pointed out. I shall argue that it is the
failure to develop a theoretical perspective which is
responsible for directing this branch of social science
towards those dead ends it seems especially prone to end
up in. My own theoretical perspective is derived from
the studies of A. Schutz (1932/67) and the symbolic
interactionism of G.H. Mead (1934).

Before we progress further let me explain my understanding of those terms. Symbolic interactionism is
simply a convenient name given to G.H. Mead's account of
how people interact with each other. In short they
understand each other through symbols - typically and
fundamentally through the symbols we call words. In
'Classrooms Observed' I wrote (Nash, 1973, p.41):

   These symbols are the guides to action that members of
   a society follow; the direct guides (norms), the
   guides to actions we ought to do (ideals) and the

subjective guides to individual actions (attitudes).
These symbols are meaningful in so far as men are able
(most of the time) to predict each other's behaviour
and to gauge their own behaviour according to the
expectations they believe others to have for them.
We can add a little more to this. The passages which
follow will elaborate the concepts of norms, ideals and
attitudes and demonstrate their centrality to the theory
of interaction which is developed.

NORMS, IDEALS AND ATTITUDES

Norms are the socially upheld rules which govern behaviour. Some of these will have the status of statutory
law, others only the status of custom, and yet others
the status of both custom and law. Within British family
life, for example, a man and woman may live together
without being married but their behaviour is not customary. A man may even set up house with two women, which
is even less the custom, but only if he tries to marry
them both will he be in breach of the law. Clearly, not
all norms have the authority of law, and equally, not all
laws are upheld as social norms. To some people it seems
quite acceptable, for example, to drive at 40 mph in
built up areas and to 'fiddle' the occasional 'phone call
or odd roll of sellotape from the office. Generally
speaking jurists like to keep legally regulated norms in
line with what is customary or acceptable in the community. This is why laws are being constantly added to and
removed from the statute book. All norms are enforced
by the application of sanctions of one sort or another
upon those who violate them. Legal norms are enforced
in a highly formalised manner by the police, judicial and
penal systems. Customary norms are enforced by less
institutionalised but often more powerful sanctions. For
example, a young couple who do live together without being
married will most probably come under some pressure from
their parents, relatives and even neighbours.
   The distinction between legalised norms and customary
norms usefully points up a matter of some interest to
sociologists. The law assumes one common community and
sanctions will be applied to anyone found guilty of
breaking the law. It doesn't matter very much whether
he knows of its existence or not. Customary norms,
however, by no means assume one community, on the contrary they are commonly specific to one particular sub-
culture or group co-existing within the larger state.
Commonly the norms of these groups can only be enforced

by sanctions which assume that those they are directed
against wish to remain members of that group. An example
might be provided by the newly elected councillor who
discovers that one or two of his colleagues are less than
perfectly scrupulous in declaring their financial interest in matters before them. An honest man himself he
mentions his concern to a friend. The friend advises
him that this is not uncommon, that it has always gone on,
that no real harm comes of it and that publicity would
only damage the image of the council and, in all likeli-
hood, ruin his own chances of advancement. These con-
siderations could quite possibly lead our new councillor
to revise his standards a little so as to remain in
favour with the group. If he decides that he no longer
wants to belong to the group then clearly these sanctions
can no longer be imposed on him.

Sociologists are especially interested in sub-cultures.
In particular there are evident normative differences
between socio-economic groups and these have been the
subject of extensive study. The business of learning
social norms begins in very early childhood. The child
is first socialised into the norms of his family, then
into the norms of the school, and - more or less simul-
taneously - into the norms of his peer group. These
three social entities are considered to be the main
socialising agencies in the child's life.

Ideals, the guides to actions we ought to do, are
learned in a similar way from our social environment. If
they are to be held distinct from norms we must say that
a failure to live up to our ideals can subject us to no
other sanctions than those stemming from our own conscience. Ideals are, therefore, by definition, set
higher than the customary norms within a particular society. For example, within Christian societies a man
might believe as an ideal that he should give all that
he has to the poor but, it scarcely needs to be said,
this isn't the normative thing to do. No one will casti-
gate him for failing to meet his ideal. We might say
that norms are enforced by others whereas ideals are
enforced only by oneself. To the extent to which we
fail to meet the ideals of our society our own conscience
is responsible. A man may hold ideals derived from various sources. Many ideals have a religious basis, others
are political and many are specific to a particular sub-
culture or group.

The concept of attitudes is particularly difficult to
pin down. We saw above that it refers to the subjective
guides to individual action. To say that an attitude is
subjective indicates that we are concerned with the

personal meanings which an individual places upon his
actions. Sometimes we find attitudes directly expressed
through words, at other times we note attitudes expressed
through bodily stance or gesture. This latter sense was
the original meaning of the word attitude. Understanding
attitudes in everyday life is very much a matter of
'reading between the lines' in other words, of interpreting the subjective meaning of the actions of another.
Attitudes can be understood as the characteristic mood of
an action. If we observe a man driving on the crown of
the road with one arm around his girl friend and within
feet of the car in front, we should take that as an
indication of his careless attitude towards driving.
Attitude is often used where 'opinion' or 'belief' would
be more accurate. Most so-called attitude tests are, in
fact, opinion tests - but more of that later.

INTERACTIONIST THEORY
AND PERCEPTION

Interactionist theory holds that in any given culture
people in a social relationship act within the taken-for-
granted framework of what things and events are considered relevant to that culture. Interaction takes place
within the context of a set of background expectancies
shared by each. Recently, 'expectations' has been used
by empiricist psychologists in a much broader sense as an
explanatory concept for teacher-pupil interaction processes. Their research will be examined in a later chapter. The theory is very much concerned with the idea of
the self. One may be as metaphysical about the self as
one likes but so far as this account is concerned, the
self is understood as a taken-for-granted proposition.
That is to say that in any social interaction I take for
granted that the other has a reflective self and a self-
consciousness of just the same sort as my own. The self
then, - the self-conscious knowledge we all have of our
personal history, our present existence, and our projected future - emerges as a result of social interaction.
How the infant develops a consciousness of himself as an
independent being is a fundamental concern of theorists
in this field. For what a person believes about himself
will form part of his motivational structure. That is to
say that a person will choose to act or not to act in a
given way because he regards himself as the sort of
person who does or does not act in that way. For example,
a man who rejects a suggested course of action saying,
'what sort of person do you think I am?' is clearly

giving as his reason for his decision his idea of himself.
These beliefs about the self are often called self-
concepts or self-images. At this point we may examine
the processes by which individuals conduct their face to
face interactions.

The following discussion of relevant theory can only
be short and will be limited to the paradigm case of
face-to-face social interaction between two people.
Quite clearly there may be interactions which are not
face-to-face, (for example, those which take place by
telephone or by letter) and which involve more than two
people; but these are special cases and will here be
ignored. Less clearly it has to be pointed out that not
all interactions can be called social interactions. Max
Weber (1922/64) has given the example of two people who
crash into each other whilst riding their bicycles. This
is obviously an interaction but it is not a social interaction although the situation might give rise to one if,
for example, the bicyclists start to talk to each other.
A social interaction exists where one person acts towards
another with the expectation that the other will respond
or notice. Within any particular social interaction
there will be a certain range of expected responses. We
can see this if we look at a very brief but successful
social interaction. A man says, 'Good morning. Bit
chilly today' to his neighbour as he goes off to work and
he expects a similar sort of reply. He expects neither
to be ignored nor to be treated to a technical discussion about the weather nor to an account of why, for his
neighbour, it is not a good morning at all. Fortunately
his neighbour understands all this and replies, 'Good
morning, John. Yes, bitter isn't it?' and drives off.
Of course, this is a highly ritualised situation and one
bounded by habit but it is a genuine social interaction
and has all the features that characterise less structured interactions. It is successful because both
persons correctly perceive the expectations of the other.
These perceptions are highly important.

Perception is much more than seeing. All sighted
persons can see but they don't necessarily perceive what
they see and, to take the contrary case, blind persons
are certainly able to perceive (albeit with input from
one less sense than most of us) what is going on around
them.

As a technical term of psychology 'perception' is
defined somewhat differently: in this context we may
understand the word to mean 'construe' or, even more
simple, 'note'. The emphasis is on perception as an
active process. Suppose, for example, that I enter a

friend's living room. At once I know that something about
the room is different from the way I saw it last. I perceive, first, that something has changed. For a moment I
am puzzled, then, 'Ah, you've taken out the old lights
and put that neon strip up.' I perceive, second, by a
deliberate act of perception, what that difference is.
In this sense perception is the active process of taking
notice of subjectively meaningful phenomena.

What sorts of phenomena people find meaningful is
another problem. To the men greeting each other as they
go off to work in the morning the entire interaction is
full of taken-for-granted meaning. Each takes for granted
that the interaction takes place within the context of
scores of similar past interactions. Let one aspect be
different and each man's perceptual mechanism will pick
up what is out of the ordinary. It might be something
very minor, perhaps one man isn't wearing his suit. That
will be noticed. One man drives off in a different
direction from usual. That will be cause for a comment.
Or it might be something more important, one man rushes
out of his house and into his car without a word, his
face flushed and his fists clenched. All this, we can be
quite sure, will be perceived instantly. For any of
these perceived deviations from the normal the other will
try to find meanings. Perhaps the man's suit is at the
cleaners. Perhaps he is trying to avoid the jam at the
roundabout by going via the overpass. Perhaps he's had a
blazing row with his wife. Whatever actions of the other
we perceive that are outside our taken-for-granted frame
of reference, we seek to give meaning to. What we have
next to consider is the adequacy of these meanings.

THE ATTRIBUTION OF MEANING

To begin with it is necessary to understand the distinction between the terms 'action' and 'behaviour'. Behaviour refers to non-deliberate movements of the body.
Blinking, reflex movements, habitual routines performed
absent-mindedly, gestures performed without awareness are
all examples of behaviour which do not have the status of
action. Action is behaviour which is subjectively meaningful and is characterised by an intention or aim. In
other words action is orientated to the future and that
future orientation can be known only to the actor himself.
In discussing this point, Weber gives the example of a man
chopping wood. One may observe a man chopping wood but
one cannot, by observation alone, determine his motivational context. Is he chopping wood for his fire, in

order to fulfil his obligations to the lumber company for
which he works, in order to test the efficiency of his
axe, or in order to become proficient for a part in a
film? Clearly these are different actions and the wood-
chopper may during the course of a morning move from one
motivational context to another without there being any
external sign. If we wish to know the meaningful grounds
of the man's actions then it is necessary to know a lot
more about the contexts in which they take place. Suppose, to take a further example, that I drive to work in
the morning, the intention of my action is to arrive at
work, and the span of the act covers the whole period of
my journey.

It is also possible to relate action to the past. So
that I may say, to use the same example, that I am driving
to work because some time ago I accepted this job. These
motivational contexts, those orientated to the past and
those projected into the future, are different in kind
and have important implications for problems of social
causality. The essential point, for the purpose of this
argument, is that reasons orientated to the past are not
sufficient to define an action or to render it fully comprehensible. Schutz, whose elaboration of the 'in order
to motive' and the 'because motive' has made significant
contribution to our understanding of human action, shows
how this distinction is most relevant to the discussion
of social causality.

IDEAL TYPES AND
SOCIAL CAUSALITY

The discussion of motivational contexts and the definition of action has a direct relevance to the scientific
understanding of social phenomena. Research can be seen
as an attempt to provide a conception or model by means
of which certain aspects of the world may be better understood. In sociology these models are known as ideal
typifications or ideal types. Weber, whose work made
clear the significance of ideal types in social science,
argues that to study, for example, the functions of
bureaucracy, we need to first delineate all the defining
characteristics of bureaucracy: to construct, in fact,
an ideal type of bureaucracy as a tool for the analysis
of actual bureaucracies.

The adequacy of a social science to explain relationships between social events rests upon the accuracy of
its ideal types to reflect reality. The ideal types
constructed by educational writers and the way in which

they change over time makes fascinating study. Consider
the different ideal type constructions of the Spens
Report (Board of Education, 1938) with those of the
Newsom Report. Spens set out three ideal types of child:
the academically minded, the technically minded, and the
practically minded, and for each of these three types
separate schools were recommended - grammar, technical
and secondary modern. The Newsom Report (Central Advisory Council for Education, 1963) presented a new ideal
type - the Newsom child - for whom non-academic courses
were to be designed. Moreover, this ideal type was
further subdivided into three others, the Robinsons, the
Browns and the Joneses. The differences, as I intend to
show by this example, between the ideal types of social
science and the personal ideal types of individuals are
ones only of degree. Incidentally, some writers use the
term stereotype to mean an ideal type inadequately
grounded in data. To them stereotype is an ideal type
constructed on prejudiced and biased grounds.

The predominant interest of the social scientist has
been to find the causes of social phenomena. In educational sciences, for example, researchers have wanted to
account for the cause of the relative failure of children from low socio-economic backgrounds in the educational system. They have concentrated on discovering the
antecedent causes of these observed social facts. However, individuals are motivated, as we have seen from
our discussion of Schutz's work, by reasons which are
orientated towards the future. This apparent paradox is
resolved by the construction of ideal types which possess
motivational structures orientated towards the past. The
most preferred model in educational sciences is the
classical input-output scheme. This model assumes causality between observed social phenomena and constructs
ideal types which provide explanatory meaning for this
causality. The implications of this are discussed more
fully below.

A theory of social interaction is necessary in so far
as we suppose that personal processes are responsible for
effects which cannot be adequately explained by a study
of more general social facts; and it is worthwhile in so
far as it deepens our understanding of the subjective
meanings of individuals and leads to the construction of
objective ideal types which give explanatory meanings to
social phenomena. The study of general social phenomena
depends upon the objective measurement of the social
phenomena concerned. Where highly general phenomena like
social class and attainment are concerned the operational
definitions employed in the construction of measurement

scales have a degree of stability approaching those of
the measures of physical science. But this is only true
of general phenomena. A scale of socio-economic status,
although specific to one culture and one time, nevertheless has a greater useful life than measures of opinion
which are often specific to a sub-culture or group which
may exist as such for only a relatively short period.
This is why we cannot expect a so-called scale of attitudes such as, to take a specific example, the Minnesota
Teacher Attitude Inventory, constructed in the 1950s
after work with teachers in the United States, to have
much meaning for British teachers in the 1970s. It is as
if in the world of physics it was necessary to redesign
the thermometer every so often to match unaccountable
alterations in the boiling and freezing points of water.
This is one explanation of why psychologists in particular are so very concerned with constructing new tests.
It is necessary because the older a test becomes the less
it reflects changing reality. In a sentence people and
societies are dynamic whereas any standardised test is
static.

The process of constructing operational definitions is,
in fact, the process of constructing ideal types. The
normal procedure is for the tester to have in mind a
personal ideal type which he wishes to objectify oper-
ationally. He will identify on the basis of his personal
ideal type a set of people (whom he will call subjects)
who are held to match that ideal type. They are given a
set of items made up by the researcher again on the basis
of his personal ideal type and from the replies a test is
constructed which objectifies that personal ideal type
and purports to measure any other person's approximation
to it. One of the most serious objections to this procedure is found in the divergence between the original
personal ideal type based on a commonsense understanding
of reality and the objective ideal type derived from the
test results.

An illustration of this is provided by the work (discussed more fully in chapter three) of those who study
teacher interaction by a standard system which involves
categorising the teacher's speech as 'direct' or 'indirect' in its effect on pupils. Early research, believing
that teachers who acted towards their pupils in an authoritarian or directive way would achieve less good
results than teachers who acted more democratically or
indirectly, studied teachers who seemed to them to be
either directive or indirective on some unstated grounds
and observed these sets of teachers so as to abstract
what seemed to be the differences between them. At this

point the distinction between behaviour and action is
lost. The researcher is no longer interested in understanding the intentions of the teacher - the reasons why
he acts in one way rather than another. The researcher
gives up the chance of identifying actions which are deliberate, and therefore open to immediate change by conscious deliberation, and behaviour which is non-deliberate
and only capable of being changed through a much slower
process. The differences which are observed between the
two sets of teachers are merely an adhoc collection with
no theoretical integrity. But from them ideal typifications of the 'direct' and the 'indirect' teacher are
constructed. It is now against these standards that other
teachers' performance is assessed as 'indirect' and
'direct'. These teachers have no status as individual
actors whatsoever: they are only seen as close or not so
close approximations to the ideal types.

It is substantively on these grounds that Gage (1963,
p.521) has criticised the Minnesota Teachers Attitude
Inventory. He writes:

it is crucial to note that the MTAI is a particular
kind of instrument. It is an empirically constructed
scale, with a scoring key that is essentially atheo-
retical, not permitting any logical explanation of
the responses that are 'right' and the responses that
are 'wrong' - on grounds other than that teachers selected on some a priori ground as 'bad' give the other.
Why they give one or the other, or how one response or
the other is related to good or bad teaching, is not
considered relevant, for the problem posed is not
rational understanding but pragmatic prediction. Here,
for example, is the first item of the scale; 'Most
children are obedient' if a respondent says Strongly
Agree, he gets +1; if he says Uncertain, he gets 0;
if he says Disagree, he gets -1 (the same as if he had
said Agree); and if he says Strongly Disagree, he gets
0 (the same as if he had said Uncertain). Or, here is
another item: 'A teacher should not be expected to do
more work than he is paid for' if the respondent says
Strongly Disagree, he gets +1; if he says Disagree, he
gets -1; if he says Uncertain, he gets -1; if he says
Agree, he gets 0; and if he says Strongly Agree, he
gets -1 (the same as if he had said Uncertain or Disagree).

Actually, the best way of getting high marks on this test
is to tick every item Strongly Disagree. This will obtain
a score of 56 - well above the average and probably better
than could be achieved by deliberate cheating.

None of this should be taken as an attack on the

necessity to construct ideal typifications of the things
and events which we wish to study. Rather the plea is
for a more deliberate and more explicit procedure. It is
essential that ideal types should be well-defined. The
practice of denying their existence is no protection
against the damage produced by their obscured deficien-
cies. One strongly suspects that it is the ill-thought
out operational definitions and inadequate ideal-types
that are primarily responsible for the relative failure
of much educational research. For the results of this
bankrupt methodology - it seems hardly surprising - have
been sadly few. Researchers in educational sciences have
adopted one new testing procedure after another and all
to little purpose. Hardly any valid generalisations
about teacher style or teacher personality have stood the
test of time: and not much time either.

It is perhaps the lack of an adequate grounding in
theory that has generated such interest in the idea of
expectations. The emergence of the term as an explanatory concept stems directly from the work of Robert
Rosenthal and his collaborator Leonora Jacobson (1968).
Their study showed - to the authors' satisfaction at
least - how randomly chosen pupils described to their
teachers as 'intellectual spurters' were actually found,
when re-tested some time later, to have shown gains in
IQ significantly higher than those of a control group.
It was reasoned that this effect - it has become known
inevitably as the Rosenthal effect - happened because the
expectations held by the teachers were communicated to
their pupils and that as a direct result of having this
knowledge the pupils responded with higher scholastic
performances. We can call this the self-fulfilling prophecy model. It assumes certain propositions to be true;
first that a teacher's expectations about pupils will be
communicated to her pupils, second that the pupils will
respond to this knowledge (and not to some other unknown
factor) and third, that these processes take place without there necessarily being awareness in the consciousness of the people concerned about what is going on.

The following chapters will critically examine, as far
as possible within the theoretical framework here outlined, the predominantly classroom based empirical research into attitudes, perceptions and learning. Several
distinct traditions have contributed to this area. Within social psychology we will consider some conventional
attitudinal studies, classroom climate research, the
analytic and observational studies of P.W. Jackson and
others, the experimental studies following Rosenthal and
Jacobson, and the self-esteem research of Brookover and

his colleagues. Sociological research which has concentrated on furthering the conceptual development of educational sciences will also be discussed.

Chapter two

Teacher perception and expressed attitude

Any attempt to test the validity of the self-fulfilling prophecy must examine the propositions I outlined towards the end of the last chapter. These were, that the teacher must perceive the pupils in ways which imply expectations about their performance, that these expectations are communicated to the pupils, that they will respond to this knowledge, and that these processes take place without the teacher, at least, being aware of them. It is arguable that the last proposition is unnecessary. But little explanation is needed if we suppose that teachers knowingly expect poor performance from certain pupils and so knowingly discriminate against them. Even if this were the general case I doubt that any research worker could afford to say so - clearly the idea would be considered an attack on the professional integrity of the teaching profession and would be fiercely resisted. We had better assume, then, that these effects take place without the conscious knowledge of the people concerned.

In selecting the empirical evidence for each of these propositions I have tried to choose from an extensive literature those studies which seem representative of a particular line of research enquiry. I have certainly not attempted to give a comprehensive survey of the field. In particular there are whole areas of research into attitudes that I have not been able to assimilate within the context of this work.

What are the taken for granted aspects of a teacher's perceptual framework? What differences exist between teachers? To what aspects of the social world are these differences related? What methods can be used to disclose their existence? It will be remembered that in considering a teacher's perceptual framework we are not concerned with his opinions or attitudes. However, although the theoretical distinctions can be made clear

the methodological procedures for investigating perceptions, attitudes and opinions tend, in practice, to be
virtually identical, and I shall draw on studies of
attitudes and perceptions as seems to me best. Most
empirical research has been concerned with the effects of
teacher expectations on pupil behaviour. There is an
obvious reciprocal hypothesis: pupil expectations and
their effects upon teacher behaviour. Very little
research has been done in this area and in these first
chapters I shall concentrate on the major proposition, in
a later chapter the perceptions of pupils will be considered in some depth.

TAKEN FOR GRANTED
PERCEPTIONS

To study the teacher's perceptions of his pupils correctly we need to know what aspects of the pupils' being the
teacher takes to be significant and meaningful. Any
study must, therefore, be concerned with asking teachers
as individuals, to tell us how they see their pupils. I
argued above that individuals actively seek to give meanings to the unusual and out of the ordinary aspects of
their environment and that these aspects are selected
from the taken-for-granted background. A sociologist
interested in studying teacher perception must necessarily get to know this taken-for-granted background.
While on teaching practice a few years ago I was asked by
my supervising teacher whether one of the boys in the
class I had just taken had been wearing a tie. I replied
that I hadn't noticed. 'Well,' he said, 'you're only
just starting. You'll soon learn to notice these things.'
To this teacher a child not wearing a tie stood out from
the rest as if he had two heads. To me wearing or not
wearing ties was of no relevance in my scheme of perceptions and I had no cause to give it attention. To the
teacher, children in correct school uniform were part of
the taken-for-granted background and any deviation was
immediately perceived. As a student teacher I did not
share these taken-for-granted elements of the situation.
What is taken for granted in one cultural setting is
extraordinary in another. In moving from a student
culture to a secondary school culture I had brought a set
of background expectancies which were no longer relevant
and which were out of place in the new setting. Any
social group - say a group of teachers in a particular
school - develops its own social norms, its own patterns
of normative behaviour, and its own set of relevancies.

Our idea of what is obvious and meaningful is learned
through our interaction with others in the cultural sett-
ings we find ourselves. My supervisor clearly expected
me to learn to see things the way teachers in that school
saw things.
   Becker (1952) was probably the first sociologist to
investigate teachers' perceptions using the only method-
ologically correct procedure - listening. One of the
teachers Becker saw said this about her pupils at a
Chicago school (reprint, p.123):
   Now the children at Z here are quite nice to teach.
   They're pliable, yes that's the word, they're
   pliable. They will go along with you on things and
   not fight you. You can take them any place and say
   to them, 'I'm counting on you not to disgrace your
   school. Let's see that Z spirit! And they'll behave
   for you. ...They can be frightened, they have fear in
   them. They're pliable, flexible, you can do things
   with them. They're afraid of their parents and what
   they'll do to them if they get into trouble at school.
   And they're afraid of the administration. They're
   afraid of being sent down to the Principal. So that
   they can be handled.
If we examine this statement carefully we can see embedded in it a set of implicit assumptions about the nature
of the children in her class. It is possible to list the
terms she uses in her description of the pupils together
with the implied opposites against which they are being
favourably contrasted:
   nice to teach   -   not nice to teach
   pliable   -   inflexible
   go along with you   -   fight you
   can be counted on   -   can't be counted on
   care about disgracing   -   don't care about
   school   disgracing school
   will behave   -   won't behave
   can be frightened   -   can't be frightened
   afraid of their parents -   not afraid of their
                                 parents
   can be handled   -   can't be handled
It seems reasonable to accept this as an indication - if
not an actual account - of this teacher's perceptual
framework when looking at children she teaches. We can
understand that she will notice and pay attention to the
actions of her pupils which can be construed within this
scheme. The situation in which she has found herself -
a Chicago (state) school in an upper working-class area -
has given rise to a taken-for-granted attitude embedded
in this particular social setting. Becker is especially

interested in showing how teachers in different social
class areas develop different taken-for-granted attitudes
and corresponding perceptual sets. This is something to
which we will return.

An early attempt to look at teachers' perceptions of
their pupils was made by Hallworth (1962). He asked
teachers from different sorts of secondary schools to
rate each pupil in their classes on twelve so-called
personality dimensions. Computer analysis revealed two
major dimensions which were called 'extraversion' and
'reliability and conscientiousness'. Most interestingly
Hallworth showed that teachers' perceptions of the
'mature' child differed according to whether they taught
in a grammar or secondary modern school. But he had to
conclude (p.130):

> not all teachers are alike in the way in which they
> classify their pupils and give meaning to the words
> they use to describe these traits. There must be
> considerable individual differences in the extent to
> which teachers make use of the dimensions that have
> been described.

Clearly, it will not be possible to examine the self-
fulfilling prophecy in process unless we can relate the
perceptions of individual teachers to the behaviour of
individual pupils.

Other researchers are moving towards naturalistic
methods: methods which rely more on examining the attitudes of individual teachers as they express them than on
their answers to conventional attitude tests. Jackson,
Silberman and Wolfson (1969) asked primary school teachers to recall the pupils in their classes. When all had
been listed the teacher was asked to describe in her own
words the first named and the last named pupils. These
descriptions were analysed to reveal the extent of the
teacher's personal involvement with these pupils. There
weren't too many important differences, though teachers
had more to say about, and seemed more involved with,
boys than girls, but the authors' methodological conclusions are worth noting (p.27):

> the results of this investigation indicate that
> differences in a teacher's personal involvement with
> her students can be detected with moderate ease in a
> brief, impromptu interview of the type she might have
> with a fellow teacher. Moreover, these differences
> are apparent whether these teachers are discussing
> those whose names first came to mind or those they
> mention last when asked to recall the membership of
> the class. The use of this naturalistic data-gather-
> ing procedure would seem to hold special promise for
> the future conduct of educational research.

THE REPERTORY GRID TECHNIQUE

One standardised procedure for investigating individual
perceptions which retains this naturalism is the repertory grid technique invented by G.A. Kelly (1955). Personal construct theory bears a general relationship to
the interactionist approach I have outlined above and
this is not the place to discuss the differences between
them. Kelly's theory assumes that each person perceives
the events and people he takes to be relevant to his life
through a repertoire of bi-polar personal constructs –
these terms are explained below – and the theory is inti-
mately related to a methodological technique. The basic
method has been refined and adapted in several ways, as
Bannister and Mair (1968) have reported, but the original
method still best explains the rationale.
    In 'Classrooms Observed' I discussed how this method
was successful in revealing the constructs employed by
primary and secondary school teachers in their perceptions
of their pupils. The teacher was presented with three
cards each bearing the name of a child in her class. She
was asked to show how one of the pupils differed in some
significant way from the other two. The teacher might
reply, 'John, now he's a pretty bright boy, but this pair
are a bit dull.' From this information we assume that
Bright – Dull is part of the teacher's perceptual scheme.
It is something she takes into account as relevant to her
task. This procedure is repeated until the teacher can
think of no more of these two ended scales: or, in Kelly's
terms, until her repertoire of personal constructs, as
they relate to her pupils, is exhausted. This is usually
after eight to twelve separate constructs have been
elicited. In this research I went on to use these constructs as rating scales to show which pupils were more
or less favourably perceived. Let me present the constructs of one primary school teacher as an example:

vivacious	–	subdued
mature	–	immature
demanding of attention	–	undemanding of attention
able to be left alone	–	unable to be left alone
well-behaved	–	poorly behaved
quiet	–	noisy
independent	–	gang member

This Scottish junior school teacher's perceptual
scheme is quite different from that of the Chicago teacher quoted by Becker. The American teacher is much more
alert than the Scottish teacher towards threatening and
disruptive behaviour. The perceptual scheme of the
Scottish teacher is orientated towards the personal qual-

ities of her pupils, their maturity, vivaciousness and
independence. She certainly does not perceive any of her
pupils as 'can't be handled' and 'afraid of parents'.
The American teacher thinks it is just as well that her
pupils are afraid but we may reasonably assume that the
Scottish teacher would be worried if her own children
were so fearful. We can relate these differences in part
to their separate individualities and in part to the
different times and cultures in which they live. We can't
decide from this limited data which part is the greater.
Larger scale studies, however, give some useful information about the relationship between the perceptual framework of an individual and the social system in which he
lives.

SOCIAL INFLUENCES ON
TEACHER PERCEPTION

Goodacre (1968) in her study of infant teachers and their
pupils' home backgrounds found that infant teachers saw
the 'good' home as one which facilitated the teachers'
task by preparing the young child for the classroom both
socially and educationally. Goodacre became interested
in teachers' perceptions of the 'good' home because she
discovered that while teachers' assessments indicated
that children in middle and upper working-class areas
were much better able to read than children in lower
working-class areas the superiority of these pupils was
not found when reading ability was tested by standardised
procedures. In other words, the working-class pupils did
better than one might have expected if the teachers'
assessments had been taken at face value. The teachers
who took home background into account were older and
expressed authoritarian opinions. Goodacre gives some
interesting facts on the type and quality of the data the
teacher takes into account when perceiving a child as
'low social class'. Conversations, class 'news', and
observations of a child's clothes (including underclothes)
and other personal belongings, were all considered relevant. These perceptions were least accurate in areas of
low social class, probably, as Goodacre says, because the
teachers were largely unfamiliar with the degree of
responsibility or training in manual occupations, unin-
formed about the nature of newer professions, and had
predetermined ideas about the type of work associated
with particular regions.
  In one small study of my own I was able to show that
there was no relationship between perceived social class -

a social class estimate derived from the repertory grid
procedure - and actual social class. Moreover, although
actual social class was not correlated with ability
measures, perceived social class was correlated not only
with the estimates of ability, but also (though less
highly), with an objective measure of ability. This
study involved only four teachers and a hundred or so
pupils - but it adds weight to the argument.

Further indication of the influence of the social
situation upon the perceptual schemes of individuals comes
from MacIntyre, Morrison and Sutherland's (1966) survey of
opinions among Scottish primary school teachers. Teachers
in different social areas were found to have distinct
aims. On the whole it seemed that teachers in working-
class areas saw their main purpose as being to concentrate
their efforts on hard-working children in order to get as
many as possible into a grammar school for a chance to
move into a non-manual occupation. In middle-class
schools teachers seemed to concentrate on pupils they
liked most as being personally pleasant. These different
aims were assumed from the opinions the teachers gave
about 'pupils worth taking trouble over'. In the sub-
urban working-class and mixed areas he (no differences
were found for girls) is pleasant and trustworthy whereas
in urban working-class areas he is attentive and hard-
working. We can suppose that these findings reflect -
if inadequately - that the perceptual schemes of the
teacher are related directly to his social situation.

There is sufficient evidence here to demonstrate the
dynamic interaction between a teacher's perceptual scheme
and her membership of a particular group. The members
of societies existing at different times and places have
different aims, different histories, different commonsense realities, and bring up new members in their own
ways of constructing reality. It can be assumed that a
teacher's perceptual scheme will function to pre-select
and construct what is reality for him, and will, therefore, be expressed in some form as attitudes in his
interactions with his pupils. If a child's actions are
perceived as, for example, 'misbehaviour' or as 'signs of
immaturity' then it is reasonable to assume that the
teacher's expressed attitudes may be communicated to the
child who may respond in ways which fulfil these expectations. Of course, a child who perceives the teacher's
attitudes towards him will not necessarily do so in her
terms. Indeed, a child is unlikely to understand that
particular actions of the teacher in relation to himself
are expressions of her perception of him as 'immature',
rather he will see the teacher's actions as indications

that she 'has got it in for me' or perhaps as a not
wholly realised perception that the teacher treats him
differently from certain of his classmates. His reactions to this situation are likely to be ones which re-
affirm and strengthen the teacher's original perception.
It is now time to examine the proposition that expressed
attitudes are communicated through interactions with
pupils.

INTERACTIONS TRANSMIT ATTITUDES

Two important studies have shown how teachers do act
differentially towards their pupils. The earliest,
Jackson and Lahaderne's (1967) paper, did not relate
observed differences in teacher-pupil contact to teacher
perception, but is, nevertheless, a seminal research.
The authors spent an average of nearly ten hours in
observation of four sixth grade (eleven years) classes.
They counted teacher-pupil interactions, noting who
initiated them, and coding each according to whether the
message was primarily instructional, managerial, or pro-
hibitory. The sheer number of interactions is impressive.
In each classroom there were, on average, a total of 109
interactions every hour. Of these 80 were instructional
(concerned with curriculum content), 14 were managerial
(concerned with procedural rules), and 15 were prohibit-
ory (concerned with discipline). The differences between the classrooms in the number of instructional
messages were not large but some classrooms had three
times as many disciplinary and managerial messages as
others. Jackson and Lahaderne comment (p.206):

> If each of these rates were multiplied by the number
> of hours in a school year (approximately 1,000), the
> absolute differences among the four classrooms would
> become quite striking. Thus over the year a student
> in Classroom A might witness as many as 16,000 more
> disciplinary messages than might a student in Class-
> room B. In room A, when the teacher turns to a mis-
> behaving student and says, 'If I've told you once,
> I've told you a thousand times...' he probably means
> it.

Almost all of these disciplinary messages were directed
to boys. In one typical classroom 108 of the 120 repri-
mands were addressed to one or another of the 17 boys in
the class. Particularly interesting was their observation that in each of the classrooms there were great inequalities in their distribution of teacher-pupil

contacts. In each classroom there were one or two children who had fewer than one interchange an hour with the
teacher while a few students had so many that, if the
contacts had been equally distributed throughout the day,
they would have been in contact with the teacher every
five or ten minutes. Some pupils might well have been in
a class of a hundred for all the attention they got,
whereas others had as many interactions as if they had
been in a class of only a dozen or so. It is evident
that knowing that a child is a member of a class of thirty
tells us very little about the social density of the
child's psychological world and the relative importance
of the teacher in that world.

This work has been taken further by Garner and Bing
(1973) who categorised verbal teacher-pupil interactions
in five infant classrooms. In addition the teachers
rated their pupils on attitude scales, and data was coll-
ected on social class and non-verbal IQ. The average
hourly teacher-pupil contacts in the five classes ranged
from 94 to 142, figures similar to those of Jackson and
Lahaderne. There were the same inequalities in the distribution of teacher-pupil contact, too. In one class
three children received 26, 24 and 23 teacher initiated
work contacts while others got 2, and one none at all.
A computer was used to 'cluster' the pupils into groups
similarly regarded by the teacher and having similar
contact patterns. These clusters closely resembled the
'attachment', 'concern', 'indifferent' and 'rejection'
attitude groups identified by Silberman.

Silberman (1969), working in the same tradition as
Jackson, asked primary school teachers four questions
designed to identify children in their classes towards
whom attitudes of attachment, concern, rejection and
indifference were expressed. The attachment question,
for example, read, 'If you could keep one student another
year for the sheer joy of it, whom would you pick?'
Three children were chosen by each teacher for each question. From the remainder of the class two control children were selected at random. Each class was observed for
some 20 hours and the teacher-pupil contacts counted and
analysed as either positive or negative evaluations, and
acquiescence (that is the percentage of pupil requests
for assistance or permission that were granted). The
results are of considerable interest. The attachment
group received more positive evaluations and more acqui-
escent replies. They did not receive more contacts. The
rejection group experienced frequent negative contacts
but they did not receive less praise than others.
Silberman argues that the teacher takes into account the

expectations of the pupils that she should display neither overt favouritism nor excessive rejection, and so suppresses her spontaneous wishes to interact less frequently with those she rejects. The teachers did, in fact, attempt to gain a measure of rapport with rejected pupils by praising them, but these efforts were countermanded by very frequent critical remarks. No strong constraints from the pupils act to modify the teacher's expression of indifference or concern, and in this area she is free to act as she wishes.

A follow-up study, using the same four attitude groups, but a more complicated interaction analysis system, was conducted by Good and Brophy (1972). Teachers of young primary school children were asked to name the pupils in their classes who fell into each group; attachment, concern, indifference and rejection. Similar results were obtained. The attachment group sought out the teacher more often than the others about matters related to work, they conformed to disciplinary norms and so were chastised less often. They received more praise and less criticism although, since their answers to questions were more often correct, this difference need not imply bias. Nevertheless, these children did get more reading turns and were asked more questions requiring conceptual thought. The concern group initiated contacts with the teacher but were less accurate in their work and preferred to guess rather than remain silent if unsure. They got more opportunities to ask questions and were sought out more often by the teacher for private conversations. They were not praised or criticised more often than others but there was a tendency for teachers to praise them more often for success and to criticise them less often for failure. The indifference group were passive, initiated fewer contacts with the teacher, and preferred to remain silent rather than to guess. The teachers did ask them as many questions as the others but they did not seek individual contact with these children nor were they called upon to run errands and the like. Even though the school performance of this group was similar to that of the others they were seldom praised or criticised. The rejection group were very active, sought out the teacher frequently, called out in class and got a great many disciplinary contacts. They also got fewer reading turns and the teacher responded less to their work efforts.

An earlier paper by Good and Brophy (1970) showed how differential teacher expectations might be communicated to pupils in ways which would tend to cause them to produce reciprocal expectations. As an indication of

teachers' 'expectations' they used a rank order of ability
provided by the teachers of four classes of 6 year-olds
who made up their sample. ~~It is at least arguable that
a teacher could rank a child as near the top of the class
and yet expect him to deteriorate. However, this is
perhaps so unlikely that the operational definition can
be accepted.~~ In each class the six children at the top
and the six at the bottom (three girls and three boys in
each case) were selected for observation. All teacher
interactions with these twelve pupils were counted and
analysed. The 'highs' sought out the teacher more often
and initiated more interactions than 'lows'. They also
got more correct answers, more praise and less criticism.
There was tendency for the teacher to initiate more contact with the 'lows' but most of this extra portion was
criticism. The teachers consistently favoured 'highs'
over 'lows' in demanding good performance. If a 'high'
gave an incorrect answer he was less likely to be criticised and the teacher would probably re-phrase or repeat
the question. When a 'low' gave an incorrect response
the teacher typically gave the answer or turned to another child. Specifically, for correct answers 'highs'
were praised more often than 'lows' (ratio 2:1), and
criticised less often for wrong answers (ratio 3:1). The
research confirmed previous findings that boys received
more interactions than girls, with the excess being largely made up of disciplinary comment, though it was suggested that this need not imply bias since teachers did
criticise girls in the same situation as they criticised
boys, but girls didn't often get themselves into these
situations. One final observation is worth noting (p.
373):

> it is of great interest that the ... teacher who
> showed the lesser discrimination between highs and
> lows was the teacher who did not group her children
> by achievement in her classroom seating pattern.

This is exactly in line with results from my own work
referred to below.

ATTITUDES ARE INTERPRETED
BY PUPILS

Research attempting to show that individual pupils do
recognise and respond to their teachers' expressed attitudes has been sparse. My own studies in this field have
been fully described in 'Classrooms Observed' but it might
be worth briefly outlining one or two findings again. I
asked children between 8 and 11 in three classes to say

(by pointing to cards bearing their classmates' names)
which children in their class were better than themselves
and which worse at, for example, reading or number work.
It was possible from this information to derive a rank-
order of self-perceived ability. Within each class this
proved to be highly correlated with a rank order of ability given by the teacher. I suggested that children
seated in homogeneous groups - that is 'streamed by
table' - were more accurate in estimating their positions
than children in classrooms where mixed ability methods
were practised. If the teacher has a 'backward reader'
table we can be pretty sure that every child in the class
will know this even if, in a vain attempt to camouflage
the meaning of her grouping, the teacher refers to it as
the 'red table' or the 'blue group'. In this study I did
not ask the children about other perceptions they had of
their teachers' behaviour towards them.

One man who has done this is Silberman, whose paper
was mentioned above, after finding that the teachers in
his sample did express their attitudes behaviourally, he
went on to discover whether their pupils were aware of
what was going on. He therefore interviewed the six
observed children in each class asking each one to compare himself with the other five on four questions concerned with contact, positive and negative evaluation,
and acquiescence. To investigate their perception of
positive evaluation Silberman asked, 'Does she ever say
things to you like "good" or "excellent" or "that's fine
work", or "I'm proud of you"? Whom does she say these
things to more, you or (name)?' On comparison questions
a student could answer 'the same' if he felt unable to
chose between himself and another student. The accuracy
of these predictions of the behaviour they would receive
was measured by correlating them with scores derived from
the observed behaviour of the teacher. Students were able
to predict better than chance the relative amount of contact, negative evaluation, and acquiescence they received.
They did not predict the relative amounts of positive
evaluation, but this may have been due to its low frequ-
ency and small variance. Students were also able to
predict the relative amounts of negative evaluation and
acquiescence received by their classmates. Silberman
stresses that a teacher's remarks, although aimed at one
individual, are heard by all, and have the effect of
guiding the perceptions of, and behaviour towards, those
students by their peers. This last point is brought out
by a further research of my own. I asked each child in a
class of thirty-four 12 year-olds to make a rank order of
ability for the pupils in the class. This gave two ranks,

one giving the self-perceived positions of each child,
the other giving the position of each child as it was
collectively perceived by his peers. Both ranks were
correlated with each other and with the teachers' estimate of ability. It seems clear that within every classroom there is a considerable degree of shared perception
among teachers and pupils.

So far we have established that a teacher's perceptions
of individual children may be translated into expressed
attitudes, and that these may be recognised by the pupils.
One element, the most vital, is still missing. There is
no evidence here that the recognition by pupils of these
attitudes directly affect their school attainment.
Garner and Bing (1973, p.241) have also noticed this and
they write:

> The data cannot resolve this 'chicken and egg' dil-
> emma, but it might be reasonable to assume that the
> process is interactive: an impression is formed on
> the basis of a child's behaviour which then acts as an
> interpretive framework within which subsequent behav-
> iour is construed, which in turn leads to teacher
> expectations which in turn helps to determine the
> child's subsequent behaviour, etc.

It would have been possible for Silberman to have asked
those children who correctly perceived their teachers as
either rejecting or seeking contact with them whether
this awareness affected the way they did their school
work. It might have been possible to persuade the teacher to alter her behaviour and to see whether the pupils'
achievements were affected. Research along these lines
could possibly clarify the causal processes which at the
moment are obscured.

I have begun by concentrating on individual processes;
the perceptions and expressed attitudes of individual
teachers towards individual pupils and their responses.
If the self-fulfilling prophecy does operate it must be
demonstrated by observation of the process with small
samples. However, most research has been concerned with
the behaviour of groups of teachers towards groups of
children and these studies must be discussed. As a start
we will examine those which attempt to establish the
causal link between teacher perception and pupil performance by experimental procedures.

Chapter three

Teacher expectation and experimental research

THE EXPERIMENTER BIAS EFFECT

The now classic experimental study of Rosenthal and
Jacobson (1968) into teacher expectations has already
been mentioned in chapter one. It is a study with a long
history. Rosenthal's concern with the experimenter bias
effect began with animal studies which apparently demonstrated that an experimenter's bias could affect the performance of animals on simple learning tasks. One early
study, Rosenthal and Jacobson (1964), involved small
teams of students working with a laboratory rat on a var-
iety of learning problems. Eight teams were told that
their rats were specially bred to learn quickly and
another six that their rats were specially bred for dull-
ness. In fact, these so called 'bright' and 'dull' rats
were randomly drawn from a homogeneous sample. At the
end of the study the 'dull' rats were found to be perfor-
ming less well on at least some learning tasks than the
'bright' rats. The students were not closely supervised
and they may have incorrectly recorded, or even fabricated
some responses. But it seems that the most likely explanation lies in the sort of handling the rats got from
the students. Students with 'bright' rats said that
their animals had received frequent gentle handling.
Whereas the students with 'dull' rats admitted to handling their rats brusquely. If this is so, we have found
that students will tend to 'pet' rats they believe to be
bright with the result that these animals will perform
better at learning tasks. Extrapolated to the classroom
situation the corollary is that teachers may 'pet' bright
children with similar results. But that question, of
course, will be treated separately.
    Another fascinating study by experimental psychologists
involved the use of the Rorschach (Ink Blot) test. Seven

students learning to administer the Rorschach were persuaded that one measure of skill in successful testing was
the number of animal responses elicited. Each student
tested two subjects who did, in fact, produce more animal
responses than normal. The testing sessions were tape-
recorded and analysis of the tapes showed that this result
could not have been due to comments by the tester. Two
possible causes were put forward. First, when a student
gave an animal response the card was taken from him, but
if he did not give a desired response it was left with him
a little longer. Second, the tester may have been comm-
unicating his satisfaction with animal responses by smiles
and bodily gestures.

Over the last ten years or so scores of experiments
like these have appeared in the journals. By now few would
doubt that there are many proven examples of the experimenter bias effect. But it is certainly true that studies
are often difficult to replicate with success. In large
part the difficulties are due to the lengthy chain of cir-
cumstances which must logically exist in order for the
effect to be demonstrated. These conditions have been
most clearly spelled out by Barber and Silver (1968,p.125):

(a) The student experimenter attended to the expectancy
communication from the principal investigator. (b) The
experimenter comprehended the expectancy communication.
(c) The experimenter retained the communication. (d)
The experimenter (intentionally or unintentionally)
attempted to transmit the expectancy to the subject.
(e) The subject (consciously or unconsciously) attended
to the expectancy communication from the experimenter.
(f) The subject (consciously or unconsciously) comprehended the experimenter's expectancy. (g) The subject
(consciously or unconsciously) retained the experimenter expectancy. (h) The subject (wittingly or unwitt-
ingly) acted upon (gave responses in harmony with) the
experimenter's expectancy

When one researcher, repeating another's work, fails
to get the same result it may be that the chain has
failed at some point. And, since any replication involves a different set of people, this is hardly to be won-
dered at. This built-in problem of replication must be
held in mind throughout the following discussion of relevant research. Despite these difficulties there is some
agreement that experimenters' expressed attitudes act to
alert the person (or animal) he is working with towards
an awareness of his, the experimenter's, attitudes. The
cues may be intentional or unintentional. To alert intentionally in this situation is tantamount to cheating
and will be ignored. Results may be misjudged or mis-

recorded, favourable comments can be passed on desired
responses, the tone of voice, facial expressions and gestures can all act to alert the subject.

EVIDENCE FROM SURVEY RESEARCH

With this background it was fairly predictable that
Rosenthal would turn his attention to the operation of
the self-fulfilling prophecy in education. It is certainly no new idea. Both Jackson (1964) in his examination of streaming in primary schools and Douglas (1964) in
a long and careful survey of social influences on children's school performance, suggested that a self-fulfilling
prophecy held by school teachers operated against working-
class children and in favour of middle-class children.

In the previous chapter I mentioned some findings of
Goodacre (1968) which showed how teachers' unfavourable
attitudes towards working-class children seemed to dep-
ress their reading performance. Recently, Pidgeon (1970)
has reviewed a large number of survey researches and has
reported several studies which seem to show a quite clear
relationship between what teachers expect and what pupils
achieve. Two of these studies are particularly interesting in the context of this discussion. Burstall (1968)
working with the National Foundation for Educational
Research studied the attitudes of teachers towards the
teaching of French to low ability pupils. Some of the
teachers had very unfavourable attitudes indeed. A
quarter of them agreed that 'Teaching French to low ability pupils is a criminal waste of time.' After two years
all the children were given an aural test of comprehen-
sion and the low ability children (those who did poorly
on other attainment tests) were divided into two groups.
The 'high' group scored above the average of all children
and the 'low' group scored very much below this average.
Burstall showed that children of very much below general
ability, who nevertheless did score above the average on
the French test, were concentrated in schools where teachers expressed favourable attitudes. Similarly, the low
scoring group were found in schools where teachers had
unfavourable attitudes and where, incidentally, inspectors had described the teaching as 'pedestrian and apathetic'.
   Pidgeon (1970) reports an NFER study in which two
groups of children took the same examination from different types of school after having taken a similar examination from the same type of school - thus providing a
unique opportunity to assess the influence of school type

on pupils' test performance. The local education authority concerned administered standardised tests of arithmetic, English, and intelligence to its primary school
leavers as part of the 11-plus procedure. Most of the
children who failed to obtain a grammar school place went
on to modern schools where a proportion of them were allowed to take the examination a second time as over-age can-
didates a year later. For administrative reasons some
primary school children who had failed the examination
were allowed to remain in their primary schools and also
given the chance to re-sit the examination a year later.
Just over 1,000 children were involved with about a quarter remaining in the primary schools and the rest moving
to the modern schools. It was thus possible to study the
effects of different types of schooling on test performance. It was clear from the analysis of the results that
children who remained at primary school were at a distinct
advantage over those who had been transferred to modern
schools. In all tests the primary group made significant
increases and the modern group significant decreases.
Pidgeon gives an example to illustrate how great these
differences are (p.63):

> Consider two 'average' children, each with a score of
> 475 on the first year's testing, and thus both 'border-
> zone' children; one stays in the primary school and
> the next year scores 490 - a clear grammar school
> place; the other, whose birthday may have been on July
> 31st, only one day older than the first child, goes to
> a modern school, and the next year scores 461 - a
> score which does not even entitle him to be considered
> as a 'border-zone' candidate.

These facts certainly entitle one to question the validity of the assumption that the performance of children
on standardised objective tests will be unaffected by
differences in the curricula they follow. It has been
shown that differences in curriculum and teaching styles
in primary schools may affect pupils' test scores. It
may also mean that similar factors affect the performances of children attending different primary schools or
different secondary schools. If this were true - and it
does seem very likely - then it makes the whole business
of selecting children for different educational provision
on the basis of such tests look very dubious. It would
mean that all astute parents who made sure that their
children went to a school with a good record in examination passes in the belief that they would stand a better
chance of success were right. And all those administrat-
ors and so called test experts who scoffed at their
beliefs and pointed to the entirely objective nature of
the testing procedures were wrong.

THE PYGMALION EXPERIMENT

These survey researches have in an indirect way shown the
importance of teacher attitudes and expectations. But
none have - nor in the nature of things could they have -
demonstrated how the attitudes and expectations of individual teachers may have affected the learning of individual pupils. Nor has this research resolved the question
of how these attitudes and expectations are communicated
in the classroom. It was for these reasons that Rosenthal
and Jacobson conducted their experiment.

An ordinary state elementary school was chosen in a
socially and racially mixed area near San Francisco. They
chose approximately 20 per cent of the children of three
classes in grades 1-6 (6-12 years). Teachers were told
that these 'special' children could be expected to show
'intellectual blooming' in the next few months. At the
end of the first year the 'bloomers' had gained significantly more points of IQ relative to the control children.
To a substantial extent this was due to changes in one
first grade classroom where the 'bloomers' improved their
relative IQ by 15 points. There were no significant gains
for grades 3-6. Indeed, in only two of eighteen classes
(one first and one second grade) did 'bloomers' show any
significant increase in IQ. In one third grade class they
even deteriorated. Nevertheless, Rosenthal and Jacobson
did conclude that they had demonstrated expectancy effects
between teachers and pupils and they speculated on the
reasons (p.180):

> Teachers may have treated their children in a more
> pleasant, friendly, and encouraging fashion when they
> expected greater intellectual gains of them. Teachers
> probably watched their special children more closely,
> and this greater attentiveness may have lead to more
> rapid reinforcement of correct responses with a con-
> sequent increase in the pupils' learning. ... Such
> communications together with possible changes in teach-
> ing technique may have helped the child to learn by
> changing his self-concept, his expectations of his own
> behaviour, and his motivation, as well as his cognitive
> style and skills.

'Pygmalion in the Classroom' became one of the most widely
publicised studies educational research has ever seen. It
came at the height of public concern in the USA about the
apparent failure of the enormously expensive pre-school
compensatory education programmes in urban areas. It
seemed to give credence to the suspicions of many radicals
that white middle-class educators were, in part at least,
themselves responsible for the very poor performances of

urban children in the school system. But in some circles
the work became infamous. Although many grassroots workers felt they had at last conclusive evidence of a phenomenon which haunted them for a long while, harder heads
were more critical. In particular Snow's (1969) review
brought out some disturbing features of Rosenthal and
Jacobson's interpretation of statistics. First among
these was the nature of the intelligence test scores used
in the research. According to the class teachers who
administered the tests (itself a dubious procedure) the
average IQ of the first grade pupils was 58. This is
about low moron level. Were the children really function-
ing so poorly? There is no evidence that they were and
one can only conclude that the test was inadequate. In
any case the instrument used, the Test of General Ability
(TOGA), has no norms below 60 and it is evident that some
unjustified extrapolations were made. Thorndike (1968)
was even more scathing and wrote of the study, 'It is so
defective technically that one can only regret that it
ever got beyond the eyes of the original investigators.'
Most psychologists probably accept the justice of these
criticisms - certainly it is hard to accept seriously
research based upon such questionable methods - and
'Pygmalion in the Classroom' is perhaps best accepted as
a pioneer study - a way of saying that although it was
far from perfect it stimulated a lot of activity. It was
certainly followed by several thought provoking papers
which avoided the worst errors of 'Pygmalion'. Of these
(I shall discuss four which obtained results supporting
the self-fulfilling prophecy and two which did not)
Palardy's (1969) is particularly ingenious.

STUDIES WHICH FOUND A TEACHER
EXPECTANCY EFFECT

Palardy identified five first grade (6 years) teachers
who believed boys to be almost as good as girls at learning to read and five others who believed boys to be only
about half as good as girls. All the children concerned
were from middle-class homes and scored above the average
on pre-reading tests. Boys and girls had very similar
scores. However, when the pupils' actual reading performance was tested, after some time with their teacher,
those boys taught by teachers who believed their potential
to be almost as good as girls did, in fact, learn as well
as girls. But boys who had been taught by teachers who
believed their potential to be greatly below that of
girls, learned noticeably less well than the girls in

their classes, and, of course, less well also than the
boys who had teachers who believed in them. Other compar-
isons also indicated the effect of teacher expectancies
and the authors suggested that their findings could be
stated in terms of the self-fulfilling prophecy (p.374):

> when teachers ... believed that boys are less success-
> ful than girls in learning to read (when they defined
> a situation as real), the boys in their classes were
> far less successful than the girls (the situation was
> real in its consequences). Conversely, when teachers
> reported that they believed that boys are as success-
> ful as girls, the boys in their classes were as succ-
> essful as girls.

Beez (1968) carried out an experimental work during a
pre-school (Head-start) programme. Sixty first grade (6
years) children and the same number of 'teachers' took
part. The children were randomly allocated to one of two
ability groups (the volunteer participants in the programme were all experienced teachers). For each group a
faked psychological dossier was prepared. Although identical in most respects the so-called 'high ability' group
was described in favourable terms and the 'low ability'
group in unfavourable terms. Before meeting his pupil
each teacher was given the dossier appropriate for his
child. The teachers worked with the children on simple
word learning tasks. Teachers of 'favoured' pupils
taught more symbols (ratio 2:1). Specifically, 87 per
cent of 'favoured' pupils learned more than eight symbols
but only 13 per cent of 'unfavoured' children learned so
many. These differences are highly significant. Analysis of tape-recordings made of the teaching sessions
showed that teachers of 'unfavoured' pupils spent more
time explaining and giving examples. Almost as many as
two-thirds of these teachers thought the tasks too difficult whereas only one teacher of a 'favoured' child
thought this.

Rothbart, Dalfen and Barrett (1971) also gave false
information to teachers. The teachers in this case were
students in training. The pupils attended high school.
Each student teacher took four pupils in a micro-teaching
situation. The student had been told that two of the
pupils were 'lacking in intellectual potential'. Analysis of tape-recordings made of these sessions showed that
the 'teachers' spent more time with 'high expectancy'
pupils. They also rated 'high expectancy' children as
intelligent and having greater potential than others.
The 'low expectancy' pupils they rated as having a need
for approval.

One other study which ought to be mentioned concerns

teachers' expectations for black students. Rubovits and
Maehr (1973) set up experimental lessons involving 66
undergraduate women on a teaching course and 264 seventh
and eighth grade pupils of mixed ability and race. Each
'teacher' was given four students of the same ability,
two of whom were white and two of whom were black. One
white child and one black were randomly given high IQs
and labelled 'gifted' thus setting up an 'expectation' to
which the teachers' responses could be studied. The
teachers were told to pay special attention to this information and to remember that they were dealing with a mixed
ability group and should be alert to differences in interest, verbal ability and so on. Each lesson (on the
subject of 'television') was observed for 40 minutes. The
observation schedule took account of six items of teacher
behaviour; teachers' attention to student statements,
encouragement of pupil statements, elaboration, ignoring,
praise, and criticism. The teachers were also given a
scale of authoritarianism. The results confirmed the
researcher's fears. Fewer statements were requested of
blacks than whites, blacks were praised less and criticised more often. There were no differences in amounts of
pupil initiated interaction. More statements were requested from 'gifted' students who were also criticised
more. The teachers quite clearly favoured 'gifted'
whites, 'non-gifted' whites, 'non-gifted' blacks and
'gifted' blacks in that order. For example, the average
amounts of teacher attention to requested statements was,
white 'gifted' 11, white 'non-gifted' 6, black 'non-
gifted' 5 and black 'gifted' 4. Similarly, the average
amounts of teacher praise were, white 'gifted' 2.0, white
'non-gifted' 1.2, black 'non-gifted' 1.5 and black
'gifted' 0.6. The authors comment (p.125):

> A pattern begins to emerge in which the expectation of
> giftedness is associated with a generally positive
> response of teachers - if the student is white. For
> black students, if anything, a reverse tendency is
> evident in which the expectations of giftedness is
> associated with less positive treatment.

Goodness knows if the findings of this study reflect a
state of affairs which is generally true in American
schools. There are no comparable studies to confirm or
disconfirm its results. The 'teachers', of course, were
not real teachers but students who might or might not
behave in the same way after the completion of their
training. They were, in fact, young idealistic middle-
class girls who expressed liberal beliefs but who had,
for the most part, no previous encounters with black
children.

These studies - and others could have been mentioned -
all support Rosenthal's basic hypothesis that teachers'
expectations for their pupils are behaviourally expressed
and result in measurable differences in learning. But
several other studies have not shown an expectancy effect
and it would be quite wrong to ignore these negative results.

STUDIES WHICH FAILED TO FIND
A TEACHER EXPECTANCY EFFECT

One thorough investigation, Claiborn (1969), failed to
find any evidence for expectancy effects. In this study
twelve first grade (6 years) classes were divided equally
into 'bias' and 'non-bias' groups. In the 'bias' groups
teachers received a list of some 20 per cent of the students who could be expected to show 'intellectual blooming'. Of course, these students were chosen at random.
Two months later re-tests showed no relative gains in
learning among the experimental group and no changes were
observed in the teacher-pupil interactions. The author
concludes, reasonably enough, that this failure to replicate the findings of Rosenthal and Jacobson points to the
need for further research before the expectancy phenomenon is accepted as a psychological fact.
    Fleming and Anttonen's (1971) study also failed to
show expectancy effects. The study involved thirty-nine
teachers of 7 year-olds. The entire sample of more than
1,000 children was divided into four groups. Different
information about the tested abilities of each of these
groups was given to the teachers: (i) traditional IQ
scores, (ii) IQ scores inflated by 16 points, (iii) no IQ
score, and (iv) Primary Mental Abilities Test (a sort of
intelligence test but not expressed as a quotient). The
children were tested at the beginning and at the end of
the study. The hypothesis, that children with inflated
IQ scores would show greater relative gains in learning
than others, was not upheld. There were no significant
differences of any kind. In passing, the authors won-
dered why, since not even knowing an IQ score made any
difference, schools bothered with testing at all. On
the question of expectancies they comment (p.251):
    The way in which teachers influence pupil behaviour
    appears to be a far more subtle and complex phenomenon
    than some have suggested. The body of knowledge and
    attitudes of teachers about testing, their personal
    characteristics and their ways of dealing with child-
    ren seem to be far more critical for pupil growth than

intervention per se. The present study suggests that teachers assess children, reject discrepant information, and operate on the basis of previously developed attitudes towards and knowledge about children and tests.

SOME COMPLICATING VARIABLES

It may be too soon yet to try to evaluate the results of the expectancy research, perhaps the only clear knowledge we have gained is an understanding that the whole subject is a great deal too complicated even to be conclusively resolved by experimental procedures. We know that expectancy effects can be found and that they cannot always be replicated, we know that the most subtle experiment may fail to show expectancy effects and we know that they will turn up (contrarily) in quite unexpected contexts. The attention given to the nature of the experiment as such suggests some additional complicating variables. These have been discussed by Schultz (1969) and Friedman (1967). They point out that most psychological experiments are performed on college students (and mostly male psychology students at that) who are most certainly not representative of the general population and perhaps not even of the student population. The student is also becoming more sophisticated. He may not know the exact purpose of the particular experiment he is taking part in, but he does know that it is probably not what the experimenter says it is. That psychologists normally mislead their subjects is so widely known that many of them pit their wits against the experimenter and even give deliberately wrong or random answers. Their suspicions are discussed with others and rumours about the experiments pass from one person to another and all act to bias the results.

One of the strangest aspects of the experimental situation is its great power over the subject. In America, at least, it seems that people will do almost anything they are told by an experimental psychologist. Orne (1962) in a revealing study gave subjects reams of paper filled with columns of random numbers which they were instructed to sum. The subjects' watches were taken from them and the experimenter left saying he would return 'eventually'. Five hours later they were still working. Milgram (1965), seeking just how far people would go in an experimental situation, had volunteers from the street give electric shocks to other volunteers whenever those others made a mistake in the task they were occupied with. Some people, under the direction of the experimenter,

gave shocks of several hundred volts. The shocks were
not real but the volunteers giving them certainly believed they were. Several cried and protested to the experimenter but seemed unable to break off the experiment and
leave the laboratory. These strongly felt constraints
have been called by Orne demand characteristics since
they demand from the subject conformity and obedience.
The recognition by researchers of these external variables has led to a new concern with the prevailing methodology and realisation that the psychologist cannot regard
people as objects in the way a physical scientist regards
his experimental material. The psychologist is not a
detached observer, he is in fact, a participant in the
experiment.

In time this revised view of the psychological experiment might lead to a clearer understanding of how the
expectancy effect can be put to good purpose in education.
This is an interesting idea. It has been assumed by most
researchers - including Rosenthal and Jacobson - that the
expectancy effect is on the whole harmful. It is unfair
in that it raises the achievements of highly thought of
pupils and lowers the achievements of poorly thought of
pupils. The highly achieving pupils get an extra bonus
and the poorly achieving ones an additional handicap.
But it must be possible to work the bias the other way.
One can imagine a situation in which teachers were actively encouraged to counteract their natural biases by
deliberately acting in positive ways towards the pupils
they think unlikely to succeed. Perhaps they might in
this way make an anti-self-fulfilling prophecy of their
expectancy and make of it a virtue. The message for ordinary teachers is that, unexplored, taken-for-granted
assumptions about pupils' potential are possibly influencing their interactions with their pupils in ways which,
for some, at least, will be unhelpful to them. And we
can suppose that a teacher who is aware of her attitudes
and who has made herself conscious of how they influence
her actions is more likely to give all her pupils equal
opportunities within her class.

Chapter four

Classroom climate

X DESCRIBING CLASSROOM
ATMOSPHERE

We have seen how two distinct research traditions - the
recent empirical research into teacher-pupil contact and
the experimenter bias effect - have both contributed to
a better understanding of the central problem of attitudes
and learning. There is a third line of research which we
must also consider. Classroom climate (or atmosphere)
refers to the overall characteristic mood set by the
teacher and the pupils in a particular classroom. We
have all been to school and we can all understand what
the terms mean. The two extracts which follow are taken
from notes made in two primary school classrooms and are
meant as a reminder of what the moment to moment reality
can be like. In both classrooms a handwork lesson is
going on and except for a few minutes towards the end of
the second lesson only the boys of each class are present:

Room A

All the boys cluster about the teacher to look at a
book on the 'Wild West'. She tells them that they are
going to make a model of the area shown in the book.
There are going to be papier mache hills and cardboard
waggons with cocktail-stick axles. A boy suggests
using match-boxes and the teacher accepts this as a
good idea. Some boys are finishing their English work.
Others get on with a mural frieze with Wild Bill Hitch-
cock and other characters. Teacher organises them,
'You get out the paints and paint them while he's
cutting out the waggons. That striped paper will do
fine. Now, Douglas, will you cut out the flames to
stick on here? You're going to make the fires. One
here and one there. Now, let's clear this away. Take
down the stuff about Barnaby Street and 'Pilgrim's

Progress' there. Now we've got a space. You can draw
all the guns they used and the clothes and things.
Yes, and George, will - wait a minute - George, these
will be better with longer ones. Yes, cut out those
like Alan's doing. Now, John, - now one of you has
got to make a mountain man. Who is going to do that?
Alistair? Good. Right, I'll give you all a wee practice. The title is, "How a Mountain Man Dressed".'
Teacher skims the text and the children make notes as
she comments, 'Well, he wore a fringed hunting suit
and trousers. Do it in your own words. And they wore
moccasins - Indian moccasins - and long hair and long
beard. No need to write it up properly. Coon skin
hat - and he'd carry a Kentucky rifle and a powder
horn. Now, he'd travel hundreds of miles to the trad-
ers down the mountains to sell his furs.' Teacher sits
at Ian's desk as she tells him this... Other boys are
scattered about the room drawing, painting, and cutting
out. They work quickly and everyone is busy. Other
children have spilled out into the corridor where they
are working at a table out of sight of the teacher.
She now gets up and gives Douglas a job to do. He is
cutting out wheels for the waggons and the teacher
finds him a container to draw around. There are two
others with him and the teacher reminds them that the
back wheels are bigger than the front ones and shows
them how to draw the spokes carefully. ... The children do not seem to notice when the teacher leaves the
room. They continue working interestedly. A group
forms around the waggon makers in the corner who are
discussing the relative merits of each other's waggons
but no other sign of the teacher's absence is noticeable.
Room B
Girls go off to sewing. The boys are handed their
various handwork jobs. A few painting, one or two
others are reading. Some have got some cards with
balls of wool to make tea cosies. There doesn't seem
to be a class project. Teacher goes around asking,
'What are you doing?' of each boy not obviously busy.
Two are sent to wash their hands. Two boys on the
floor look pretty happy painting a Mickey Mouse style
elephant. Most boys are sitting at their desks. Teacher stands over the boys painting. He is pretty
sharp with them. 'I think it is a pity you made the
blue so dark.' The boys look at their painting and
shrug as the teacher turns away. The boys at the far
table are not doing any handwork at all. They are
thinking up names of cars and writing them down. This

is a game. They go round the table each taking a
letter in turn and writing down a car name beginning
with that letter - Lamborghini, Morris, Nash, Opel -
and so on. Teacher ignores them. Teacher talks to
the boys painting, 'Where did you ever see a black elephant? I said shades of grey. And you're going to
have a hole through that paper.' The room is a bit
subdued. At one table four boys have a pile of plasticine and a few scraps of cotton wool. One boy is
squeezing it flat with his ruler. Another boy pokes a
lump with his pencil. I ask what they are doing.
'Don't know,' they say, 'we started making animals then
canoes but they didn't work. Do you know what we can
make?' Three boys take a model - it looks like an
inverted pyramid on a plasticine stand - to the teacher.
'What's that supposed to be?' he asks. The children
stand around looking defensive about it. The teacher
says, 'All right, let's have all this stuff cleared
away, we'll have the girls back soon.' Boys pack away
their things. Only some half dozen of the twenty boys
in the class have been engaged in any kind of creative
activity.... Teacher leaves the room. Noise level
rises sharply. Melanie, Alice and Catherine turn
around. Someone calls out loudly, 'She's a pet!'
Steve calls over the room to Tommy. He goes over to
him. Almost everyone is talking loudly and there is a
lot of shouting. Six people are now out of their seats
and walking around the room. Alice is playing at strang-
gling George. Jane and Melanie are attacking Ronald.
Alice joins in too. More shouting. Someone has apparently stuck a pin into his neighbour's back. More
children leave their seats. Two boys are playing an
arm press game. Two others join in. This catches on
very quickly and a hard struggle is soon going on at
the front bench. Several children at the back of the
room get up to look out of the window. One boy rattles
a ruler loudly on the iron rim of his desk. A couple
of girls are still apparently reading but no one else
is doing any work.
I spent some weeks as an observer in these classes and
it seemed to me that the atmosphere in room A could scarcely have been more different from that in room B. Some
clear objective differences can be picked out of the
records. The teacher in room A is continually busy organising and arranging work for the boys to get on with. Her
comments are constructive ('These axles will be better
with longer ones') and she readily accepts and praises the
boys' suggestions. The boys are so busy and so interested
in the work that they are doing that they hardly notice

when the teacher leaves the room. Indeed, a group of them
are working quite out of her sight in the corridor. It is
noticeable, too, that the teacher gets close to the children. They cluster around her to look at the books. She
sits at one of their desks to read and dictate notes. In
room B the teacher spends little time organising the
lesson and doesn't seem to notice that most of the children have nothing to do. When he talks to the children it
is usually to criticise them ('Where did you ever see a
black elephant? What's that supposed to be?') Although
he walks around the room he does not sit with the boys or
get closely involved with them. The children's interest
in what they are doing is so low that when the teacher is
out of the room almost all of the children are fighting
and shouting within a few minutes.

Observations of this sort certainly leave a strong impression of the atmosphere in the class being studied. But
the value of such impressionistic or 'phenomenological'
records is primarily heuristic. They are valuable for
describing and detailing aspects of reality in an explor-
atory manner. For the researcher who prefers to work with
less obviously subjective techniques it is clear that as a
necessary first step there have to be identified a set of
specific actions which are believed to contribute to what
is experienced subjectively as climate or atmosphere. In
such an analysis can be included the amount and quality
of the teacher's praise and criticism, her acceptance of
pupils' ideas, and her willingness to get closely involved with them. All these characteristics can be defined
in objective terms and measured by simple counting against
a check-list or with a rating scale. The main difficulty
of this approach lies in getting the researcher to agree
on a standard procedure. This line of research was initiated many decades ago and there are now literally scores
of such check-lists and analysis systems in existence if
not in use. Many of these are discussed by Amidon and
Simon (1965) and Boyd and De Vault (1966) in comprehensive
reviews.

THE DEVELOPMENT OF CATEGORY
SYSTEMS

The concern with classroom climate has an interesting
history. Lippet and White's (1943) original and influential study, carried out in wartime America, showed how
boys responded to three different artificially created
climates - democratic, laissez-faire and authoritarian.
This is a particularly clear example of how greatly social

scientists are influenced by important contemporary problems. Americans during the war were giving a lot of
thought to issues of leadership, democracy and totalit-
arianism. This is not to say that the work is propaganda
but it is worth remembering the wider context of its time.
Considering its enormous influence it was, in fact, a
rather small study involving four adults and two classes
of 10- to 12-year-old boys. The boys were divided into
fifteen 'clubs' of five boys each who met in the evening,
under the supervision of one of the adults, to make model
aeroplanes and the like. The four adults took turns to
act as supervisor each practising a different style of
leadership. The democratic leader encouraged group decision making, gave assistance, and made fair and objective
comments on the boys' work. The laissez-faire leader
adopted a passive role, he gave the boys freedom to do as
they pleased, made no suggestions, and never praised or
criticised their work. He tried to be friendly rather
than stand-offish but he did not interfere. The authoritarian leader made all the decisions, told the boys what
to do one step at a time, remained aloof and never made
clear his criteria for praise and criticism. Observers
at the meetings made very complete records including
shorthand notes of all that was said.
     The boys behaved very differently under these three
conditions of leadership. Under democratic leadership
the boys were very productive and displayed no hostility.
When the teacher left the room they carried on as before.
Boys with an authoritarian leader reacted in two different ways. A few were apathetic and did little work.
Others were hostile to other groups and to their leader.
The laissez-faire group produced very little and seemed
disorganised. One of the boys who took part in the experiment said (p.500):
     I liked RW (democratic) best, then DA (laissez-faire)
     and then RL (authoritarian). RW was a good sport,
     works along with us and helps us a lot; he thinks of
     things just like we do and was just one of us - he
     never did try to be the boss, and wasn't strict at all,
     but we always had plenty to do. DA didn't do much, he
     just sat and watched; there wasn't much I didn't like
     about him, but he didn't help us much ...not like RW
     when we had regular meetings and that was very good.
     RL was allright mostly; he was sort of dictator like,
     and we had to say what he said pretty nearly; he helped
     us work but he was sort of bossy.
Although the research was not carried out in an actual
classroom, and was never primarily intended as an educational study, its importance in stimulating interest in

classroom climate and performance is hard to overestimate.
It helped to define the basic terms in which for more than
a decade research into the relative effectiveness of the
dominant-authoritarian teacher and the accepting-democra-
tic teacher was carried on.

Of equal importance is Anderson and Brewer's (1945)
research into the teaching style of nursery teachers.
Contacts between teachers and pupils were observed and
coded as being basically dominant or integrative. In the
same way pupil-pupil contacts were also coded as dominative (snatching another's toy, striking, or using force)
and integrative (offering a choice, showing willingness to
share). Once again this was a small study involving only
four teachers but it did suggest that there was some relationship between the behaviour of the children and the
teaching style of the teacher. However, its real importance lay in the isolation of dominative and integrative
behaviours as important, in the great care with which the
observation schedules were constructed, and in its concern
with the activities of the real classroom. It led directly, though not immediately, to the important work of
Withall (1951) and Flanders(1970).

Withall developed an index of seven categories to give
an objective measure of teacher-pupil interactions in the
classroom. These were:
1   learner supportive statements or questions,
2   acceptant or clarifying statements or questions,
3   problem structuring statements or questions,
4   neutral statements evidencing no support intent,
5   directive statements or questions,
6   reproving, disapproving, or disparaging statements
    or questions
7   teacher supportive statements or questions.
This category system enabled Withall to measure the integ-
rative-dominative ratio by taking the number of interactions falling into the categories 1, 2 and 3 to the number
falling into the categories 5, 6 and 7. Clearly, this
should correspond roughly to the ratio of 'learner centred'
to 'teacher centred' statements. Perhaps the most ingenious aspect of Withall's work was his attempt to check
on the interpretations of observers using this system and
the feelings of children in the classroom. Pupils were
provided with buttons to press when they felt negatively
(or positively) and at the same time an observer rated
the statements as 'learner centred' or 'teacher centred'
according to the definitions developed for the index.
This procedure seemed to give some support for Withall's
assumption that the measurement of classroom climate in
this way was worthwhile.

Before turning to a discussion of Flanders' work it
may be worth mentioning the OScAR observation schedule
which has been widely used, both in America, where it was
developed, and in Britain. Medley and Mitzel (1958) designed the OScAR - Observation Schedule And Record - as a
method of observing and measuring classroom behaviour.
The observer first records on one side of the OScAR card
information about pupils' activities, the groupings in
the classroom, the materials and teaching aids being used,
aspects of the classroom climate, and the subjects being
taught. These observations are made over a five-minute
period. The observer next categorises on the reverse of
the card all teacher statements as, pupil supportive,
problem structuring, miscellaneous, directive, and reproving. At the same time tallies are made of instances of
behaviour expressing approval or disapproval of pupils.
After five minutes the observer completes this section
and starts over again. This alternation of sides of the
card is continued until six five-minute periods of observation are completed. OScAR does enable relatively un-
trained observers to obtain reliable information about
the differences in classrooms of different teachers. The
recent survey of Scottish primary schools by Duthie (1970)
used the OScAR to help identify items of teacher behaviour
which could be replaced or assisted by non-teaching aux-
iliaries.

THE FLANDERS INTERACTION
ANALYSIS SYSTEM

The Flanders Interaction Analysis System was designed to
provide objective data which would enable the research
worker to differentiate between indirect (democratic/
integrative) and direct (authoritarian/dominative) teacher styles. Flanders assumes that verbal interaction between teacher and pupils can be understood as a discrete
series of sequential events. Each 'event' is defined as
'the shortest possible act that a trained observer can
identify and record'. It has to be pointed out that there
is no attempt to define action as meaningful behaviour.
It is presumed that behavioural laws exist which determine the relationship between teacher behaviour and pupil
learning and that these laws may be discovered by the
analysis of objectively categorised speech. The intentions of the teacher are not considered relevant. In the
sense that sociologists use the term Flanders is not concerned with meaningful action. The system identifies
seven categories of teacher speech, four related to an

indirect style and three to a direct style. Two categories are concerned with pupil speech and one is reserved
for silence and confusion. The full category system is
as follows:

  1 Interpreting the feelings of the class,
  2 Praising the pupils,
  3 Accepting and building upon the pupils' ideas,
  4 Asking questions,
  5 Lecturing and giving opinions,
  6 Giving directions and instructions,
  7 Punishing and criticising,
  8 Pupils respond to teacher's interaction,
  9 Pupils initiate interaction and contribute own
     ideas,
 10 Silence and confusion.

This is an all-inclusive system. There are no examples
of teacher or pupil speech which cannot be coded by these
categories. The researcher observes the lesson, and,
using a specially laid out coding sheet and a stop watch,
writes down the category number of each three second
speech event as it happens. This is not an especially
difficult skill to learn. The category system can be
memorised in a matter of minutes and a few hours of practice is normally enough to acquire the correct tempo.
The observer makes additional notes so he can recall later
an outline of the lesson. An example will show how the
system is used:

  0   (Noise as children enter the room)
  6 T. All right, settle down quickly, now. John,
  6   open the window above you....
  0
  6   O.K. That's right. Books open at....
  4   Where are we? David?
  8 D. Chapter four, Miss.
  6 T. Chapter four. Page fifty-eight. Look at the
  6   picture first.
  4   What is it showing us?
  8 P. Landscape, Miss.
  4   Umm. What sort of landscape?
  8 P. Fields and things.
  4 T. What kinds of things?
  8 P. Farm buildings - sort of towers.
  4 T. Anyone know what they're called?
  8 P. I think they are silos, Miss. I think you
  9   store food in them for the animals.... So that
  9   in the winter the animals can be fed.
  2 T. Right. Well done, Alan. Anybody ever seen one?
  4   A silo?

The data - a list of numbers like that on the left of

the passage above - may be analysed to show what proport-
ions of the interactions fall into each category. We can
show, for example, how much of a lesson is spent in giving
orders and directions and so on. More importantly we can
show the extent to which a teacher uses direct and indirect categories. Usually this is expressed as a ratio
found by dividing the number of direct categories by the
number of indirect categories. Two Integrative-Dominat-
ive ratios may be calculated. The I/D ratio is the product of the categories 1, 2, 3 and 4 divided by the categories 5, 6 and 7. The i/d ratio is the product of the
categories 1, 2 and 3 divided by the categories 6 and 7.
The latter ratio is generally preferred since it is independent of drill patterns which are often characteristic
of particular subjects. Observations of social studies
lessons in American schools gave the following patterns
of interaction after several hours of recording: categories 1, 2 and 3 - 98; category 4 - 105; category 5 - 394;
categories 6 and 7 - 56; and categories 8, 9 and 10 - 348.
The numbers are in thousands. The ratios, as the reader
may check for himself, were I/D - 0.45 and i/d - 1.75.
These are the ratios of teachers classed as indirect.
Similar observations of direct teachers resulted in an
I/D ratio of 0.25 and and i/d of 0.19. It is claimed
that indirect teachers are more alert to, and concerned
with, students. They make greater use of statements made
by pupils and try to integrate their ideas into the
lesson. They ask more extended questions and receive
longer pupil answers. Direct teachers seem to have more
discipline problems, give longer directions, and have to
repeat themselves more frequently than indirect teachers.

CLASSROOM CLIMATE AND
PUPIL PERFORMANCE

A quite considerable amount of work has gone into correlating these I/D ratios with measured pupil performance.
The general idea is, of course, that teachers with a favourable (that is democratic/integrative) style will have
a higher ratio of indirect to direct categories than
teachers with an unfavourable (that is authoritarian/dom-
inative) style. Therefore, pupils whose teachers have
high I/D ratios will score more highly on tests than will
pupils whose teachers have low I/D ratios. This, at
least, is the theory. In practice the truth has proved
to be more complicated.
    Amidon and Flanders (1961) in an early paper observed
the lessons of 54 geometry teachers who were classed as

direct or indirect on the FIAS. There were few differences in the measured attainments of pupils although it did
seem that pupils who were particularly dependent on the
teacher did learn more from indirect teachers. The latest
review of this line of research by Westbury and Bellack
(1971) examined eight studies involving the correlation of
pupil attainments with teachers' I/D ratios. Their conclusions were not encouraging (p.75):

> The most liberal interpretation of the results would be
> that six of the eight studies found some statistical
> procedure which indicated a significant relationship
> between high scores on an I/D ratio and pupil achieve-
> ments measured by at least one of the attainment tests.

At first sight six out of eight seems a good enough result
but we should note that this is a generous interpretation
and means only that six of the studies were not totally
unfruitful.

The unimpressive results of research using interaction
analysis techniques have disappointed the hopes of many
workers and call for some explanation. The Flanders
Interaction Analysis System in particular has considerable
strengths. It is able to record the presence or absence
of particular types of interaction in a given period of
observation. It can record these interactions in an
objective and practical manner which preserves the original sequence of events. The data can be analysed by com-
putor and the flow of interactions in the lesson may be
displayed in ways that are immediately comprehensible even
to people unfamiliar with the system. Extensive research
with the FIAS has also provided some useful insights into
classroom practices in American secondary schools - and
by implication into British schools also. Flanders has
summarised these in his rule of two-thirds: in the classroom someone is talking two-thirds of the time, two-thirds
of this talk is teacher talk, and two-thirds of teacher
talk consists of direct influence - lecturing, giving
directions or criticising. At the moment most work with
the FIAS is concerned with teacher training. Student
teachers are being instructed in specific teaching skills
by intensive practice with small groups of pupils. In a
typical lesson a student might face six pupils for fifteen
minutes. The student's tutor uses the FIAS to provide an
objective record of the student's performance in the
micro-teaching session: a record which is almost immediately available for discussion. It is argued that in this
context interaction analysis can be a useful tool in
teacher education. Suppose that a tutor wants to help a
student talk less himself in lessons and to encourage
pupil participation. His progress can be observed over a

series of micro-teaching sessions and, hopefully, his
tally of categories 2 (praise), 3 (using pupils' ideas)
and 4 (asking questions) will rise and his tally of categories 5 (lecturing), 6 (giving directions) and 7 (criticising) will fall. There is little doubt that extended
tuition of this sort may help the student teacher to gain
important professional skills which might, in a more traditional course of teacher training, have been ignored.
The key problem is whether the skills gained through laboratory based micro-teaching - a very artificial situation - can be carried through to the reality of the forty-
minute school lesson with thirty-five pupils. As yet
there is not the least evidence that they can be. The
FIAS assumes that the teacher is primarily - or even
wholly - responsible for the patterns of interaction in
the classroom. One needs only a little teaching experience to begin to wonder about the truth of this assumption. For some reason the transactional nature of the
personal relationships in the classroom is overlooked by
interaction analysis.

The concern with teacher training probably reflects a
general recognition that the potential of simple analysis
systems to measure classroom climate has been exhausted.
It is now understood that the atmosphere of a classroom is
so much more than the amount of praise and criticism used
by the teacher. It lies partly in the quality and tone of
voice and partly in the precise words used but, more than
this, it lies in the non-verbal actions of the teacher,
how often she moves around the room, how closely she approaches the pupils, and in her facial expressions and
bodily gestures. Look back at the extracts given at the
beginning of the chapter. In class A the teacher is, in
fact, rarely seen to praise the pupils and when she talks
it is mostly to give direction and advice. On the FIAS
her pattern of interaction would appear direct rather
than indirect. The class B teacher would also appear
direct but not so very much more so. In other words the
FIAS can hardly begin to cope with the real differences
of style, vitality and concern which distinguish the two
teachers. It has to be recognised that no system of this
sort can be sensitive enough to count and measure objectively the all important non-verbal cues, which more than
verbal interaction alone, are responsible for the overall
climate of the classroom. For an additional reason for
the decline of research into classroom climate we can look
back to the researches of Jackson and Lahaderne (1967)
whose work was discussed in chapter two. The climate of a
classroom is not the same for all the pupils in the class.
What we need to know about is not the classroom climate as

it seems to the researcher, however objective he might be,
but how the quality of the teacher's interactions are perceived by individual pupils.

The FIAS assumes that the informal/indirect teacher is
likely to be the more successful and yet the technique is
only suitable for relatively formally taught lessons.
There are many primary schools where the observer simply
cannot hear what the teacher is saying. The classroom is
noisy, the teacher is talking quietly to a small group of
children at the other side of the room and the observer
using the FIAS is left recording an unbroken series of
category O (silence and confusion). But perhaps the most
damaging weakness of the FIAS (and most other systems) is
its total failure to concern itself with cognitive content. Flanders believes that if American education is not
completely successful that is due to the inadequacies of
traditional modes of teaching. He implies that the
pupils' failure to learn can be remedied by improving the
techniques and skills of the teacher - by getting the
question and answer sequence right. And in this rather
simplistic view he fails to relate to other more fundamental criticisms of American education.

Henry (1963) in a powerful anthropological critique of
the meaning of American schooling has argued that American
education fails in its stated aims because, to summarise
his conclusions baldly, there is far too much information
to teach, the teacher has no need of any of the knowledge
he possesses except only for the purpose of teaching it,
he is remote from the consequences of teaching failure,
much of his knowledge is out of date and irrelevant to
the real concerns of the community, and his own status in
that community is low. Interaction analysis is part of
this system of schooling and seeks to make it more effici-
ent. What really disturbs critics like Henry is that by
using Flanders' methods a teacher might use his enhanced
skills of interaction management to teach yet more irrelevant material and yet more wrong-headed views of the
world. But, following the best traditions of objective
science, interaction analysts don't trouble themselves
with questions of that sort.

Chapter five

Self-concept
and school achievement

The self - the self-conscious knowledge we all have of
our personal history, our present existence and our projected future - emerges as a result of social interaction.
Finding one's way through the research literature concerned with studies of the self is more than ordinarily difficult. Self theories have been developed by more than
one psychologist of major stature and at least three influential positions have inspired empirical research.
Before a particular study can be properly understood or
related to other work it is necessary to know at least
something of its underlying theoretical assumptions.
There is space here to give only the briefest mention of
the central ideas of these theories; but perhaps the
reader will be reminded how important they are as a
source of ideas.

MAJOR THEORIES OF THE 'SELF'

Freudian theory holds that during early childhood the self
develops in terms of three structures. These are the Id
(instinctual drives), the Ego (the adaptive part of the
mind which brings it into conformity with external reality) and the Super-Ego (a specialist function of the Ego
which orders the mind's energies along social paths).
Self did not assume an essential importance in Freud's own
work and it was his daughter, Anna Freud, who was among
the first to emphasise the importance of self images in
the individual. It was Neo-Freudian ego-psychology which
introduced the idea of ego-defence mechanisms - among them
projection, introjection, and rationalisation - into
everyday speech. Psychotherapists of this school believed
that it was their function to help a patient through to a
position where he could recognise his true goals and

realise self-fulfilment or self-actualisation.

Meadian theory, as it has developed, states that the self emerges through the active process of a person accepting as his own the ideas about himself he perceives others to hold. Mead calls this process 'taking the role of the other' and it describes how the child comes to have ideas about himself - self-concepts - which are similar to those his significant others have of him. A child's significant others will include his parents and those living in his home, his teachers and his school friends. Although infancy and childhood are seen as the crucial periods Mead recognises that the self develops throughout life. In adulthood significant others will include a person's husband or wife, children, workmates and so on. The term reference groups is commonly used to mean such groups of people who are perceived as significant others.

The third tradition influencing self-concept we may call empirical. It draws its inspiration from behaviourist psychology and, incidentally, is thus in a curious state of contradiction since classical behaviourism does not recognise 'self' as a legitimate concept. However, some empiricists have supposed that self-concepts are important in some way - though they make no assumptions about the origins of the self - and these investigators have contributed towards the development of techniques for measuring the self-concept in individuals. With the important exception of the NFER studies by Barker Lunn (1970) and Ferri (1971) most of the research discussed here has its roots in Mead's interactionist theory, but whatever their theoretical position all the authors accept that children's self-concepts may have a measurable effect on their school performance. In practice, researchers also tend to use very similar methods to investigate self-concept in that they accept self reports based on replies to paper and pencil tests as an adequate indication of a child's real feelings about himself. Early research studied the relationship between teachers' perceptions of their pupils' self-concepts and the pupils' own statements. Two of these studies had a particularly important part in stimulating interest among educators in self-concept research.

EARLY STUDIES OF THE
SELF-CONCEPT IN CHILDREN

Perkins (1958) set out to investigate aspects of the social climate but his paper is also one of the first studies of the self-concept in school children and it

seems reasonable to discuss it here. The study involved a
number of 10- to 12-year-old children from seven schools.
They were asked to sort fifty statements such as, 'I look
on the bright side of things', 'I understand the kind of
person I am' and 'I am not a fast runner' and to nominate
up to four classmates, including themselves, for each
statement. Teachers were asked to nominate four children
using twenty-five similar statements. This procedure is
known as the 'Q' sort technique and was widely used at
that time by American social psychologists. But even this
rather artificial methodology showed that the teachers
were as accurate as their pupils at predicting children's
perceptions of each other. Similar findings were reached
by Davidson and Lang (1960) in their study of just over
200 10- to 11-year-olds from a New York school. All the
children were assessed as having above average reading
ability. They were asked to give replies to the questions
'My teacher thinks I am...' and 'I think I am...' using a
set of adjectives provided. These gave measures of,
respectively, teacher favourability and of self-percep-
tion. The teachers also rated pupils on adhoc scales of
academic achievement, behavioural, and personality characteristics. High correlations were found between all these
measures. In other words, on these tests, the children
indicated that they perceived themselves in very much the
same way as they thought their teachers perceived them.
Moreover, those children who said they thought well of
themselves were regarded by the teacher as well behaved
and of high ability. Davidson and Lang stress the importance of the interaction between the child's self-concept,
the perceptions the teacher has of that self-concept and
the child's behaviour (p.112):

> The teacher's feelings of importance and approval are
> communicated to the child and perceived by him as pos-
> itive appraisals. It is likely that these appraisals
> encourage the child to seek further teacher approval
> by achieving well and behaving in a manner acceptable
> to his teacher. We may also begin this cycle with the
> child's behaviour. The child who achieves well and
> behaves satisfactorily is bound to please the teacher.
> She, in turn, communicates positive feelings towards
> the child, thus reinforcing his desire to be a good
> pupil. Which of these variables serves as the primary
> determinant is a fact difficult to ascertain. It seems
> rather that they reinforce each other.

Demonstrating that teachers and pupils have very similar views about how they experience events and feelings
in the classroom is a necessary first step in relating
self-concept to achievement. However, research of the

sort presented above does have serious limitations. Wylie
(1961) who reviewed several hundred self-concept studies
became noticeably frustrated in her attempts to draw together some worthwhile conclusions. Every study involved
a unique combination of assumptions, hypotheses, procedures and measuring instruments which made synthesis of the
results very risky. This is true of almost all research
in the social sciences and it need not always be a weakness. It is significant that in self-concept work essentially similar findings are reached by independent researchers even though their theoretical stance and methodological procedures may differ. Nevertheless, systematic
studies which have accumulated a substantial body of work
with a common methodological base are of special importance.

THE BROOKOVER RESEARCHES

One of the most impressive of such studies has been that
of Brookover and his associates (1965) and (1967). Brookover argues that although research in the sociology of
education has drawn attention to the relationship between
social class membership and academic achievement it has
done little to explain how the causal relationship - to
assume that one exists - operates between these factors.
Brookover, who follows Meadian thought on the importance
of the self, supposes that self-concept is the linking
factor. The Brookover team report a number of related
studies based on a six year longitudinal programme involving more than 500 American high school children aged 13
to 18 years. The children's self-concepts of academic
ability were investigated by questionnaires. The questions included, for example, 'How would you rate yourself
in school ability compared with those in your class at
school?' The pupils were asked to tick one of five following alternative replies such as (a) I am among the best,
(b) I am above average, (c) I am average, (d) I am below
average, (e) I am among the poorest. From the answers to
questions like these, received over a number of years,
Brookover was able to reach certain conclusions about the
self-concept in school children and its relationship to
achievement. Predictably, self-concept and school achievement were correlated in all grades. There is a strong
temptation to deduce too much from all this: what could it
possibly mean if children of this age really did not know
whether they were above or below the class average as the
case might be? One particularly interesting aspect of
Brookover's research concerned attempts to improve the

academic performance of a sample of poorly-achieving 14-
year-olds by enhancing their self-concept of ability.
The most successful treatment involved working with the
pupils' parents. Parents were persuaded by the research
staff not to make disparaging or negative remarks about
their children's work but always to give encouragement
and praise for any school achievement. After a time this
treatment, which went on apparently without the knowledge
of either the children or their teachers, did result in
an improvement in the children's self-concept of academic
ability and, the crucial point, a parallel improvement in
their work. This treatment proved to be more effective
than counselling the children - indeed one experimental
group who attended sessions with a trained counsellor
actually did worse in many respects than a control group -
however, even the favourable results of working through
the parents did not persist after the experimental treatment had been discontinued.

Brookover concludes that self-concept of academic ability is a threshold variable. He points out - it is an
obvious but perhaps necessary reminder - that low social
class membership cannot be a sufficient cause of poor
school achievement since it is plain that not all children
of low social class do badly in school any more than all
children from upper and middle classes do well. It is
suggested that below a certain level of ability children
will not succeed in school whatever their social class or
self-concept: but if the self-concept is low then not
even middle-class children of high ability will do well.
This is an attractive hypothesis in that it seeks for
explanations of negative cases. It has always been a
little embarrassing for sociologists who continually
stress the importance of demographic variables to explain
just how it is that some children from broken homes end
up as barristers - not delinquents, and how some children
from the East End become Conservative Members of Parliam-
ent - not barrow boys. Brookover's research introduces
the idea of self-concept as a threshold variable which
intervenes between social class and school performance
and places behaviour under the control of the individual.
Although a person's choice of action can be regarded as
being heavily influenced by background variables there is
no commitment to a theory of social determinism.

ACHIEVEMENT AND SELF-CONCEPT

The suspected relationship between self-concept and achievement can now be argued through. A child who thinks
well of himself will want to keep up his ideas of himself
(maintain his self-concept), he will almost certainly
regard the teacher as a 'significant other' and will wish
to be favourably perceived by her, he will want to live
up to the expectations she will have for him and in turn
her reactions towards him are likely to become more favourable. His parents will most probably support his efforts and he will tend to make friends with other children
like himself. In contrast, the child who does not think
well of his abilities in school will tend not to do well.
There seem to be two possibilities. He may feel ashamed
of his poor abilities and might even despair or, and it
may seem less likely, he may want to maintain his idea of
himself as someone who is not good at school work (it
could be important in keeping his status with his friends,
for example), he will probably not regard the teacher as
a 'significant other' and will be less concerned with
being favourably perceived by her. He will tend not to
try very hard in class and his teacher is consequently
unlikely to regard him with any particular enthusiasm.
His parents may not be concerned with his school work and
he will tend to make friends with others like himself.
All of these linkages can be supported by research findings. These are very tight circles and they are started
and kept going as much by the perceptions and expectations people have about each other as by their actual behaviour. But there are no inevitabilities in social
science and the probability always exists of breaking
into these circles at some point.

EVIDENCE FROM SURVEY RESEARCH

The large NFER survey by Barker Lunn (1970) also investigated self-concept. Barker Lunn's academic self-image
scale consisted of nine questions which formed part of a
much larger questionnaire. Questions such as 'I'm useless
at school.work', 'I'm very good at sums' and 'My teacher
thinks I'm clever' are representative examples of those
asked. More than 2,000 children from twenty-eight primary
schools were asked to indicate whether each statement was
true for them - most of the time, sometimes, or never.
The investigations of self-concept were seen as relevant
to the question of streaming. As the author argued, some
supporters of streaming claim that bright pupils in mixed

ability classes give daily reminders to the less able of
their inadequacies so helping to undermine those children's self-confidence, while others, with opposing views,
argue that streaming lowers the aspirations of all children, other than those in the top stream, and that the
lower stream children are led to moderate their abilities
and consequently to develop poor self-concepts.   Barker
Lunn had noted at an earlier stage of the research that it
seemed quite common for teachers not to enjoy teaching low
ability children.   One teacher remarked, in front of the
class, 'I don't like teaching dull children; I wasn't
trained to teach them.   Those are my bright children over
there (pointing to a row by the window), the average are
in the middle and the dull children are over there.'   The
children in this class could have had no doubt about their
worth in the teacher's estimation.

Barker Lunn distinguished between teachers with generally 'progressive' and 'child centred' beliefs and those
with 'traditional' and 'formal' beliefs.   For ease of reference these were called, respectively, Type 1 and Type 2
teachers.   The findings of large correlational studies
like this one are very difficult to summarise without
over-simplifying the genuinely complex results.   There
was no doubt, however, that academic ability was correlated with self-concept for all pupils.   'A' stream pupils
had a high self-image as did children who were near the
top of the 'B' and 'C' classes.   Low ability children in
non-streamed schools had a poor self-image and it seems
that a considerable number of low ability children experienced shame at their not being clever.   Apparently teachers constantly compared these children with the more able
members of their class and this had a detrimental effect
on their self-concept.   The highest correlation with self-
image was with the pupil's relationship with their teacher - a finding exactly in line with those of Davidson and
Lang, and Perkins discussed above.   As for teacher type
differences it turned out that above average ability
pupils had the best self-images when taught by Type 1
teachers in non-streamed schools.   This is just what one
would expect.   The Type 1 teachers are working within a
context they find congenial while the Type 2 teachers are
having to cope with a classroom organisation not to their
liking.   The results of their discomforture are clear in
their pupils' self-images.   There are many other findings
in this report which cannot be easily discussed out of
context.   Barker Lunn's study is more easily available
than most of the research discussed here and it needs to
be read closely.

Ferri (1971), in a follow-up study, investigated the

self-concept of about 800 children in non-streamed junior
schools and 900 in streamed junior schools who were sub-
sequently transferred to grammar, comprehensive and modern
schools.   It is worth noting that the low ability pupils
developed more favourable self-concepts in their secondary
schools.   Children who went to grammar schools developed
poorer self-images while boys who went to modern schools
improved their self-images.   Ferri suggests that the apparent drop in the self-concepts of bright children moving
to grammar schools may be explained by remembering that
in primary school they were top of the class whereas after
moving to grammar school they could no longer all hold
that position.

The NFER researches have demonstrated two significant
relationships that earlier work had overlooked.   A teacher's beliefs about teaching - whether she is 'progressive'
or 'traditional' - seems to affect the self-concepts of
the pupils in her classes.   The result of this appears to
be particularly detrimental when the teacher is required
to teach in a context that is incompatible with her beliefs.   Additionally, the surveys have indicated how central to a pupil's self-concept is his class position.   It
is not his actualability that seems to matter so much as
his ability as he compares it with others in his class.
The self-concept of children transferred to grammar
school does not rise - as one might reasonably have expected - but it drops as the children's standard of comparison rises.

SELF-CONCEPT AND
SCHOOL REGIME

One other recent British study of the self-concept was
concerned with the expectations of the headteacher.
Palfrey (1973) studied two schools, a boys' secondary
modern school and a girls'.   Both were small and each
year group was streamed into three forms.   Although the
schools were close neighbours each had a different regime.
At the girls' school neatness and orderliness were regarded as very important, the girls all wore a uniform and
the formalities of discipline were strict.   The boys generally did not wear a uniform and discipline was more re-
laxed.   Palfrey argues that the headteacher regarded the
boys as predictable products of their home environment -
a Welsh mining area - and did not expect them to have
high academic or occupational aspirations.   By contrast
the headmistress placed some considerable stress on achievement and there was a routine of prize giving, house

meetings, merit marks, school teams and so on.   Palfrey
argues that these differences in what we may call headteacher style were important factors influencing their
pupils' self-concepts. He expected that the boys would
have measurably lower self-concepts than the girls.   To
test this hypothesis a short questionnaire was given to
some sixty fourth-form boys and to a similar number of
girls. The headteacher completed a similar questionnaire. Both headteachers recognised that their pupils were
below average in ability and from working-class homes.
However, their responses differed in some important respects. The headmaster thought that his boys were only
fairly well behaved and believed that very few would get
a worthwhile job after leaving school. The headmistress
saw her girls as very well behaved and thought as many as
half of them would get a worthwhile job. It is most interesting to learn that both the girls and the boys saw
themselves more favourably than their headteachers. Over
80 per cent of boys and girls thought they were fairly
clever and 6 per cent of the girls thought that they were
very bright. But the pupils seemed to agree with their
respective headteachers about their future jobs. As many
as 55 per cent of the girls thought that they would get a
good job after leaving school whereas only 20 per cent of
the boys thought so. It has to be said that this study
has considerable weaknesses. There are no statistical
tests of the results and, more importantly, no control
groups were employed. It may be that girls believe they
will obtain better jobs than boys regardless of the type
of school regime. Ford's (1969) study of comprehensive
school children showed quite clearly that girls had mark-
edly better aspirations than boys. Despite these draw-
backs, the attempt to investigate what has long been
accepted as important - the interaction between the expectations of the headteacher and the pupils' self-images -
is certainly worthwhile.

Hargreaves (1972) has made a useful attempt to draw together in a theoretical perspective the relationship between teacher expectations, self-concepts and pupils' academic achievement. Hargreaves suggests that three variables, the teacher's conception of the pupil's ability,
the pupil's own conception of his ability and whether or
not the pupil regards the teacher as a significant other,
all have a part to play in bringing about the self-fulfilling prophecy effect. In Hargreaves' scheme the pupils
most likely to fulfil the teachers' expectations will be
those who are (a) perceived as bright by their teacher,
who perceive themselves as bright, and who perceive the
teacher as a significant other and (b) those who are per-

ceived as dull by the teacher, who perceive themselves as
dull, and who perceive the teacher as a significant other.
Those who are least likely to live up to the teachers'
expectations will be (c) those who are perceived as bright
by the teacher, who see themselves as dull, and who do not
regard the teacher as a significant other and (d) those
who are perceived as dull by the teacher, who perceive
themselves as bright, and who do not regard the teacher as
a significant other. Where the perceptions of the teacher
and the pupil are incongruent and where the teacher is not
seen as a significant other there is unlikely to be any
manifestation of the expectancy effect. Hargreaves'
scheme relates entirely to what is perceived by the teacher and the pupil. Unlike Brookover, he does not suggest
that actual ability has any part to play in the operation
of the expectancy phenomenon. So far there is no evidence
to support Hargreaves' position but his clear statement
might well serve as a basis for empirical study. The
scheme certainly offers an explanation for both the positive and the negative results of the experiments into the
expectancy effect discussed in earlier chapters. It may
be that children reported to their teachers as 'spurters'
and so perhaps treated favourably, will develop enhanced
self-concepts and improved performance provided that they
regard the teacher as a significant other. If this is
correct - and it sounds reasonable - then there is clearly
little point in attempting further expectancy studies
without taking into account the pupils' self-concepts and
the extent to which they regard the teacher as a significant other.

   In the end we can say that children's reported self-
concepts are influenced by (i) their perception of their
ability relative to others in their class (ii) the regard
in which they are held by their teacher and (iii) the
extent to which their school achievements are supported by
their parents. It would be good to know more about the
ability of the concerned teacher to improve the class work
of low ability pupils by deliberately interacting with
them in ways calculated to build up their self-concepts.
It might at least be possible to prevent the development
in children of the appallingly low self-concepts that so
many are burdened with.

Chapter six

Attitudes and expectations of pupils

The attitudes and expectations pupils have for teachers have been largely ignored by research. There seems to be a general belief that what pupils feel and think can be manipulated by the teacher. The Flanders Interaction Analysis System discussed in an earlier chapter provides a nice example of this. Only two of the nine categories are reserved for pupil interactions. Micro-teaching, which draws heavily on interaction analysis, is based on the assumption that pupils' behaviour is essentially a function of teacher behaviour. Student teachers are supposed to acquire skills which they can rely on to produce certain pupil behaviour in the classroom. There is some evidence that students can be taught particular skills, for example, how to ask 'probing' questions, how to reinforce (that is praise) pupils' correct responses, and so on. But no one has yet proved that these skills produce the same behaviour from thirty pupils in their own classroom as they do from six children in the laboratory. It is not only interaction analysis that fails to acknowledge the pupils' contribution to the patterns of behaviour in the classroom, not much is heard about how pupils see things from any area of research. Yet there are at least two reasons why pupils' opinions could be regarded as significant. First, if we recognise that teachers' expectations for pupils have an effect on the pupils' behaviour - and there is no shortage of research into that question - then we should recognise the reciprocal hypothesis that pupils' expectations for their teachers might have an effect on the teachers' behaviour. Second, although pupils' opinions about school (attitudes) and pupils' opinions about their own performance in school (self-concepts) are almost always treated by research workers as being quite distinct they are, in fact, closely related to each other and both sets of feelings - whatever

we want to call them - are related to the friendship
groups children form in school. The interest that has
been shown in pupils' attitudes has focused on two slight-
ly different aspects. Some researchers have investigated
how pupils see the 'good' and the 'bad' teacher while
others have tried to relate pupils' attitudes to school to
their actual achievements. Studies of friendship groups
have been investigated quite separately again. This pen-
ultimate chapter will look at previous research in these
areas and then attempt to integrate the findings and discuss their importance for the teacher.

WHAT PUPILS THINK
ABOUT TEACHERS

Taylor (1962) developed rating scales to measure children's views of the 'good' teacher on four categories of
behaviour, teaching, discipline, personal qualities and
organisation. The scales were developed from an analysis
of children's essays and were administered to nearly 900
pupils from several junior, modern and grammar schools.
In general, children evaluated most highly the 'good'
teacher's teaching. Pupils in streamed schools rated most
highly the teacher's discipline. These children were concerned that the 'good' teacher should be firm and able to
keep order. In unstreamed junior schools children rated
most highly the teacher's personal qualities, her patience,
sympathy and understanding. Among secondary school children it seemed that in the fourth year, boys in particular
rated most highly personal qualities such as cheerfulness,
good temper and a sense of humour. Most children rated
the 'good' teacher as being firm and fair in her discipline, having a good knowledge of the subject, able to explain difficult points and be helpful and encouraging.
   Hargreaves (1972), who has reviewed most of the pert-
inent literature, arrived at essentially similar conclusions. He argues that pupils take into account three distinct aspects of their teacher's behaviour, their discipline, their instructional style and their personality.
Under discipline children prefer teachers who keep control, are fair, have no favourites, give no extreme or
immoderate punishments, and dislike those who are too
strict or too lax, have favourites, 'pick on' pupils, and
who punish and threaten excessively or arbitrarily. Where
instructional methods are concerned children prefer teachers who explain and give help where it is necessary, and
give interesting lessons. They dislike teachers who do
not explain, give little help, do not know their subject

well, and who give dull and boring lessons. Pupils prefer
teachers whose personalities are cheerful, friendly,
patient, and understanding, who have a good sense of
humour and who take an interest in pupils as individuals.
They dislike teachers who nag, ridicule, are sarcastic,
bad-tempered and unkind, and who have no sense of humour
and ignore individual differences.
    It can't be said that these findings are unexpected.
No one is going to win a Nobel Prize for discovering that
pupils prefer their teachers to be knowledgeable and helpful rather than ignorant and unfair. But there is perhaps
a little more to it than this. One point worth noting is
that these views about 'good' and 'bad' teachers are held
virtually by all children, by those who do well and like
school and by those who do not. It is less than immediately obvious that, for example, poorly behaved children
should prefer teachers who impose a firm discipline as
emphatically as do well-behaved children. One might have
supposed that poorly behaved pupils would have preferred
lax teachers whom they could have more easily disobeyed.
All the evidence, however, suggests that this is not so.
Again, these findings are not merely descriptions of
children's likes and dislikes about teachers, they are a
formulation of the rules of conduct which children lay
down for their teachers. These attitudes and expectations develop a normative function. The class transforms
what their teachers generally say and do into customary
rules for all their teachers to follow. Interactionist
theory recognises that regular patterns of behaviour by
one person will be perceived by others as setting expectations for future behaviour along similar paths. And if
that behaviour is not produced the others will act towards the person to keep his behaviour along expected
lines. This, then, is half the story. What of the research into the relationship between pupils' liking for
school and their performance?

PUPIL PERFORMANCE AND
ATTITUDES TO SCHOOL

Jackson (1968) suggests that at least two lines of reasoning lead to the expectation that scholastic success and
positive attitude to school go hand in hand. First, traditional learning theory suggests that children who do
well in school will be rewarded which, in turn, will lead
to their developing a liking for school. This is an idea
which appeals to commonsense. And there is an argument
which reverses the causality and says that children who

like school will do well there for that reason alone,
rather as contented cows give the best milk. In practice,
as one might have begun to suspect by now, things are not
that simple. Jackson discusses six studies, including one
by himself, and only once or twice was any sort of correlation found between pupils' attitudes towards school and
their academic performance. Generally, it seemed that
although about one pupil in five or six felt strongly
enough to complain about some aspect of life in school
these were not exclusively the least able children. There
are curious contradictions. One study showed that although one group of 11-year-olds were 'happy' with their
classroom experience, about a quarter said they could do
with less of it and almost half could remember a time when
they had been happier at school. A lot must depend on the
exact question asked.

One of the earliest studies reported by Jackson was
carried out in the 1940s by Tannenbaum who investigated
the attitudes of more than 600 12- and 13-year-olds from
three New York high schools. Nearly half of the boys
liked school, a quarter were ambivalent, and getting on
for a quarter actively disliked school. Most of the girls
liked school and only a very few had ambivalent attitudes.
These findings, as Jackson shows in his discussion, have
been replicated many times by later research. Now, given
that we have attitudes towards school distributed in this
way it is pretty clear that there cannot be any very close
relationship between pupils' attitudes towards school and
their abilities. Obviously, when something like 80 per
cent or more girls say that they enjoy school then, since
in the nature of things not all of them can be of above
average ability, a fair number of poorly achieving girls
must have favourable attitudes.

Jackson himself studied the attitudes towards school
of nearly 300 12- to 13-year-olds in an attempt to clarify
some of the ambiguities. He was particularly interested
in the 'fit' between the attitudes of individual pupils
and the assessments the teachers made of those attitudes.
Teachers were generally accurate in their perceptions of
two groups, 'satisfied' girls and 'dissatisfied' boys.
They expected high IQ pupils to be satisfied with school
and low IQ pupils to be dissatisfied and in cases where
this was not true the teachers generally misperceived the
situation. In fact, teachers saw their pupils' feelings
about school to be more closely related to ability than to
anything else. Jackson argues that the logically anticip-
ated relationship between students' attitudes towards
school and scholastic success is rather difficult to demonstrate empirically except in extreme cases. There is an

inevitable clash between the desires of pupils and the re-
quirements of the school. Sometimes, perhaps often, a
pupil is not going to want to do what the school wants him
to do. Since there is not much the pupil can do about it
the only sensible thing to do is to take things as they
come and not to feel too badly about them. In this acceptance of the taken-for-granted order of things Jackson
sees the clue to the apparently curious lack of correlation between ability and attitude to school. He writes
(p.81):

> Suppose ... that a small number of students dislike
> school intensely and an equally small number are corr-
> espondingly positive in their opinion, but that most
> students have either mixed or very neutral feelings
> about their classroom experience. Perhaps for attit-
> udes to interact with achievement they have to be ex-
> treme, and extreme attitudes, either positive or neg-
> ative, may be much rarer than commonly thought.

There seems to be a lot of good sense in this argument,
but at least one recent study has found a definite relationship between academic performance and attitudes towards
school. Barker Lunn (1970) using scales developed for her
study of streaming already referred to in previous chapters, investigated children's attitudes towards both their
class and their school. Attitude towards school was measured by a scale including the items, 'School is fun', 'I
would leave school tomorrow if I could' and 'I like
school.' The attitude to class scale included the items,
'I'd rather be in my class than others for my age' and
'I hate being in the class I'm in now.' The scales correlated highly with each other. Both tests were correlated with several tests of achievement including English,
problem arithmetic, essay writing and verbal reasoning
(IQ), and even more highly with teachers' ratings of
ability. The highest correlations between both attitude
measures were with interest in school work. The correlation between this and attitude to school was 0.71 -
which is very high for this sort of research. Between
interest in school work and attitude to class the correlation was 0.43, lower, but still very significant. The
correlation with relationship with teacher was also high.

AN EMPIRICAL STUDY

Results as contradictory as these cannot be reconciled too
easily. Perhaps all that can be said is that the time,
the place, the children, and the questionnaires were different and that one or more of these differences were

enough to give findings at variance with the earlier American work. In a very recent study I have attempted to investigate how pupils' attitudes to their teachers actually set up expectations which affect the teachers' behaviour. The study involved only one class of 12- to 13-year-olds but the children were interviewed individually so that much more probing questions could be asked than would have been possible by using a questionnaire. Each pupil was presented with three cards each bearing the name of one of his teachers. He was then asked to sort the cards into two sets, (i) teachers he 'got on with' and (ii) teachers he did not 'get on with'. Ideally, the child might say, for example, 'Well, Mrs X (whom he does not 'get on with') and Miss Y are different because Miss Y helps you more. Mrs X just walks up and down.' From this it can be deduced that the pupil employs the construct behaves helpfully - behaves unhelpfully in his perception of teachers. The children were not asked to force their answers into a formal set of constructs rather they were encouraged to discuss and compare the teachers as they liked. Analysis of the conversations revealed six constructs which seemed to be commonly held by all, or almost all, pupils.
These were:

1 keeps order   -   unable to keep order
2 teaches you   -   doesn't teach you
3 explains   -   doesn't explain
4 interesting   -   boring
5 fair   -   unfair
6 friendly   -   unfriendly

Everyone agreed that teachers should be able to keep order. Pupils who were well behaved considered that the teacher should keep the noisy ones quiet so that they could get on with their work. Less obviously the noisy children also believed that teachers should keep them in order. Indeed, these children commonly blamed the teacher for being 'soft' and failing to keep them disciplined. Pupils also expected teachers to teach specific and well-defined subjects. They preferred lessons which left them with a feeling of having learned something. They didn't regard discussion periods, for example, as proper teaching. Teachers were expected to help and explain when the children were having difficulties in understanding their work. They particularly disliked teachers who told them to 'work it out for themselves' and to 'think'. They appreciated the teacher who made her lessons flow and who made the main points of the lesson clearly and in a way that they could understand. Few children enjoyed periods where the teacher continually punctuated the progress of the lesson with questions that seemed disruptive. Fairness was something all children mentioned. They expected firmness, if not strictness, but the teacher was expected to behave fairly to everyone. She should give a warning or a second chance before punishing. She should not punish all children for the faults of a few. Inability to catch the guilty ones was not seen as an excuse to blame everyone. She was not expected to have 'favourites' or to 'pick on' pupils. The children expected to be treated with a degree of equity and if they were not they would protest. Teachers were also expected to be friendly, to talk conversationally, and not to shout or domineer the class. Several children, particularly girls, said that they were often made upset and nervous by over-bearing or inexperienced teachers.

These attitudes are seen by the children as expectations of the normal standard of behaviour for their teachers. It certainly seems that the expectations pupils have for teachers have a considerable influence on the behaviour of the teachers. It was clear that the teachers the children did not get on with were those who did not keep to these expectations. With some teachers the misunderstanding can be particularly sad. I have seen several liberally minded teachers who cared deeply for their pupils but who, because they refused to follow the accepted disciplinary techniques, were unable to gain even a minimal degree of co-operation from the class. The teacher's behaviour would be seen as 'soft' and a few bolder boys would become unruly. Unable to cope with the situation the teacher's lessons become disrupted. Other children become bored and inattentive. The teacher tries to re-assert her authority over the class and threatens to have them all in for detention unless there is quiet. The pupils think this is unfair, 'I wasn't doing anything, Miss.' The teacher raises her voice and gets a semblance of order again. A few of the more nervous children begin to find concentration difficult. Wary of losing control again the teacher tells a pupil asking for help to be quiet and 'think'. The pupils start to see the teacher as unhelpful and unfriendly. The situation is almost as bad for the domineering and over-strict teacher. Very few secondary school classes will allow a teacher to be unfair and harsh without protesting in some positive way. Sometimes they will simply do no work, refuse to answer questions, or participate in the lesson. Other classes have been known to deal with unjust teachers by dropping pencils, humming or sneezing in unison until the teacher's life is so uncomfortable that he simply has to stop, if he has any sense at all, and say, 'All right, let's get this

sorted out. What's the problem?' Patterns of teaching
behaviour are negotiated by the teachers and the pupils
together. The teacher cannot just impose his or her style
on a class but must gain at least a minimal amount of co-
operation from the pupils.
   Many of the expectations pupils have implicitly recognise a passive conception of their role. For example, the
children think they should be kept in order. They do not
believe they should be given the opportunity to control
their own behaviour. Again they say that they should be
taught things. They do not demand that they be given the
opportunity to find things out for themselves. In some
ways this seems to be particularly disturbing. The conception of teacher behaviour they consider correct is one.
that greatly restricts their own autonomy and their range
of purposeful action. If the experience of school does
generate such limiting self-definitions it is arguably
failing to achieve one of its central aims.

FRIENDSHIP GROUPS

Now that we have a good idea of how children in school
perceive their teacher, and how their feelings about
school are related, or not, to their ability, it is time
to show how their expectations and attitudes are correlated with the friendship groups they form in school.
Hargreaves (1967), in a detailed study of how boys in a
streamed secondary school formed friendships clearly diff-
erentiated by ability and attitudes towards school, was
one of the first to emphasise the importance of this conn-
ection. Hargreaves gave the different classes sentence
completion tests such as, 'Teachers think of me as...'.
As many as 73 per cent of 'D' stream boys gave negative
replies, for example, 'a big bully and a great big long
haired nit' and 'hopeless' whereas only 10 per cent of 'A'
stream boys gave unfavourable replies. The attitudes of
the 'A' and the 'D' stream boys were poles apart. 'A'
stream boys enjoyed school, got on well with the teachers,
thought it was important to work hard in order to pass
their examinations and get a worthwhile job after leaving
school. On the whole they were polite and well behaved.
'D' stream boys disliked school, intensely disliked some
of their teachers, had no interest in examinations -
indeed were not due to take any - and were rude and dis-
obedient. The reactions of the staff, as one can easily
predict, were equally clearly distinct. Boys from the 'A'
stream were encouraged and favoured with various privil-
eges. They were the prefects, the school team captains

and so on. They went on the school outings and, in a
word, they were treated decently. Boys from the 'D'
stream were scarcely tolerated by the staff. They were
given odd jobs to do about the building, they were the
butt of sarcastic jibes and, all in all, got a very ungen-
erous treatment from most teachers. Hargreaves relates
this acute divergence in the attitudes of children from
different streams explicitly to the expectations of the
teachers, he writes (p.105):

> In a streamed school the teacher categorises the pupils
> not only in terms of the inferences he makes from the
> child's classroom behaviour but also from the child's
> stream level. It is for this reason that the teacher
> can rebuke an 'A' stream boy for behaving like a 'D'
> stream boy. The teacher has learned to expect certain
> kinds of behaviour from members of different streams.

The Barker Lunn (1970) streaming survey also had something to say about the structure of friendship groups in
junior schools. In particular it demonstrated how close
was the relationship between friendship, ability and
social class. The study analysed the characteristics of
mutual pairs - that is to say pairs of children each of
whom chose the other on a socio-metric test. No less
than 80 per cent of these reciprocated choices were between children either of the same social class or just one
grade apart. This was true of children in streamed and
unstreamed schools. The children were graded in four ability bands, in streamed schools 59 per cent of mutual
pairs were from the same ability band, 34 per cent were
one band apart, and 7 per cent were two bands apart. In
unstreamed schools the distribution of friendships was
not very different, 42 per cent of mutual pairs were from
the same ability band, 33 per cent were just one band
apart, and 23 per cent two bands apart. The percentages
of mutual pairs from the same ability band are about twice
what might be expected by chance.

In a study of friendship groups among 11- to 12-year-
olds I was able (Nash, 1973) to look closely at friendship
and attitudes. The sample consisted of 152 children from
the top classes of five unstreamed primary schools. In
these five classes there were 84 boys, 64 of these formed
13 identifiable cliques, of these, 6 were defined as favourably perceived by their teacher and 7 as unfavourably
perceived. Twenty boys were not members of a clique. Of
the 93 girls 72 formed 21 cliques, 11 defined as favourably perceived, leaving 21 as non-clique members. Membership of these cliques was significantly associated with
social class and IQ. There was also a tendency for age of
wanting to leave school to be associated but this did not

reach significance. Soon after these data had been coll-
ected the children were transferred to secondary school
and the new friendship choices of just one class were studied in some detail. The boys were seen to be formed into
two favourably perceived cliques, with four boys in each,
and two poorly perceived cliques, one of three boys the
other of two. There were two non-clique members. The
twenty girls in the class formed three favourably perceived cliques, one of four girls the others of two girls
each. One girl was not a clique member. The association
with IQ and age of wanting to leave school was statistic-
ally significant. Social class membership, however, did
not correlate with friendship choice though the trend was
in the expected direction. A closer analysis of the
cliques of boys will help to bring out the importance of
these cliques in patterning the attitudes of the children
towards school. The four boys who made up clique I had
an average IQ of 112. All wanted to remain at school
after the statutory leaving age. Their teachers perceived
them very favourably. The boys themselves liked school
and thought it was worthwhile to work hard although they
would often instigate noisy scenes in the classroom if
they were bored by the lesson or thought that the teacher
was unable to control them. Clique II were a group of
four boys, moderately favourably perceived by their teachers, with an average IQ of 102. Again they all wanted to
remain at school after the statutory leaving age. Although they worked hard when they were interested, and
were favourably disposed towards school, they were very
quick to react to any signs of inexperience on the part of
the teacher and could be particularly noisy. Clique III
were a group of three boys with an IQ of about 87. Two
of the boys wanted to leave school as soon as they could
and the third, though he wanted to remain at school longer
did not like school very much. This boy did not fit
easily into the group, he tended to sit quietly on his
own, and did not join in when the others were disruptive.
However, all three were perceived unfavourably by their
teachers. Clique IV were a pair of boys whose IQs were
very low. Both wanted to leave school as soon as possible. They were perceived in very unfavourable terms by
their teachers, and they themselves did not like school.
One of these boys was later transferred to a remedial
stream. I have argued that the boys in this unstreamed
secondary school class provide an almost perfect example
of the tendency for children to polarise into small
cliques. The reality of these cliques is beyond dispute.
They are revealed by the sociogram, by the report of the
teacher, and by the statements of the children. Each

clique has its own distinct attitude towards school, its
own agreed perceptions of the other cliques, and its own
pattern of behaviour in and out of the classroom.

Three different approaches have demonstrated the importance of pupils' attitudes towards school. These attitudes influence the friendship choices children make and,
in turn, those friendships act to strengthen the children's attitudes. It seems probable that the majority of
children do not have strong feelings about school one way
or the other. Sometimes they are pleased with things and
sometimes they are not, but for the most part their feelings about school are neutral. The research findings are
not completely agreed on the extent to which attitudes
interact with ability. The commonsense view that children
with either strongly positive or negative attitudes towards school will do well and poorly respectively seems to
be right. There is less doubt about the perceptions children have about the 'good' and the 'bad' teacher. Their
ideas, in fact, are little different from those the headmaster or college tutor will have about ideal teacher behaviour, able to teach, keep order, act fairly towards all
pupils, and be friendly - no one could ask more than that.
How these attitudes become expectations influencing teacher behaviour is, for me, the most interesting aspect of
the work. Here again there is the same complementary
relationship we have seen earlier, the teacher's usual
patterns of behaviour are perceived by the pupils to set
a standard for their future behaviour; in a word, pupils
expect the teachers to continue in the way that they have
behaved in the past and, having these expectations, the
children themselves act towards the teachers in ways which
act to ensure that those expectations are confirmed.

Chapter seven

Classroom teaching
and classroom research

For some years now I have been visiting schools as a research worker, observing, asking questions of the teachers
and pupils; and there is always one question I am asked in
return: 'What good is it - what practical results will
you get?' Teachers are essentially practical people and
they believe that research should be concerned with making
more understandable the problems they face. Most of us
engaged in research would agree that, in the final analysis, research in education must be related to the concerns of teachers. It must aim to make the experience of
schooling more successful for all children. Yet there are
differences between the perspectives of the teacher and
those of the researcher which ought to be considered.

RESEARCH PERSPECTIVES

Teachers tend to be interested in those questions which
confront them as problems in their daily experience. They
will consider as worthwhile research on the relationship
between the abilities of children in streamed and non-
streamed classes, the incidence of early leaving in comprehensive and grammar schools, the impact of an integrated curriculum on working-class children, the strengths
and weaknesses of a particular reading method, and so on.
These are legitimate concerns and all have been the subject of intensive research by people who have accepted
that teachers are correct to regard these issues as relevant problems. There is another aspect to research,
though, which does not accept teachers' definitions of
what issues are problematical but which treats those very
definitions as subject to enquiry.
    This might be characterised as 'looking for problems
where none exist': more open-mindedly we might say that

the concern was with 'problems about problems'. For the
last few months I have been thinking about the sorts of
judgments HMIs make in their assessment of schools. This
concern arose from a re-reading of the Plowden Report
(Central Advisory Council for Education, 1967). The
Report gives a scale of merit which the inspectors used to
rate primary schools and, curiously, the criteria which
they employ are of a particularly subjective kind. Inspectors rated some schools, for example, as 'shows signs
of life and seeds of growth' and I found myself wondering
what this could possibly mean. It is obviously metaphor-
ical - there are no actual seeds involved - and the reference is presumably to the state of the schools' organisation and curriculum. But what an extraordinary thing:
here is a government body - a parallel organisation when
one thinks about it to the factory inspectorate - which
apparently uses criteria of assessment known only to
itself and expressed in such a way that the possibilities
of misunderstanding and misinterpretation are made as
great as possible. For no one but the inspectors could
possibly use this scale - only they know what it means.
And I wonder whether they all know, and all have the same
idea? Does the inspectorate attempt to standardise its
criteria? Is there any moderating procedure so that one
HMI's assessment may be checked, systematically, against
another's? Of course not. An HMI is chosen for his experience, and his ability to understand these criteria
(and to regard them as non-problematical) is probably an
essential qualification for appointment. This is a good
example, I think, of the way in which an academic researcher is trained to look for problems - to make aspects of
the world which seem taken-for-granted by others problematical and open to investigation. It is not an easy thing
to do. The whole weight of established opinion is usually
against such an enquiry and unable to see its worth. HMIs
usually tell me at some point that should I be privileged
to spend twenty years in their job I should then have no
difficulty in understanding their criteria. Not only is
such a lengthy socialisation unlikely in my case but this
attitude is antithetical to a scientific analysis of their
work.
    The tensions between the practical knowledge for which
the teacher feels a need and the kind of understanding
which an academic researcher has to offer are very real.
One is reminded of this in small but significant ways. I
am invited now and then to address groups of teachers
following in-service courses, on some such topic as
'Teacher expectations and the ROSLA child' or 'Classroom
interaction and the integrated day'. The teachers are

there because they have an interest in ROSLA children or
the integrated day - and it is plain that they will listen
to an outside lecture only if it seems strictly relevant
to their concerns.   There is a danger, then, in allowing
research to be completely dominated by the immediate in-
terests of the people involved.   But it would be wrong if
academic research became unconcerned with practical
issues.   The bulk of the work discussed in previous chapters does have a very direct relevance to teachers.

Its central implication concerns the framework which a
teacher employs in understanding her pupils.   I have tried
to show that research into 'attitudes', 'perceptions' or
'expectations' is all essentially concerned with the same
problem: how teachers relate to pupils on the basis of a
model they have of what pupils may be.   There is no point
in expecting teachers (or anyone else) not to have 'attitudes' or 'expectations'.   It is often suggested, as an
ideal, that a teacher should regard her pupils as individuals - as uniquely different beings - and no one would
want to gainsay that.   But it misses the point that some
people are seen as individuals in certain respects because
they exhibit characteristics which make them stand out
from others who do not seem individual in those respects.

HOW SUBJECTIVE IDEAS BECOME
OBJECTIVE FACT

One problem with all ideal typifications of a subjective
kind is that they are never fully explicated.   A teacher
may regard certain of her children as 'bright' by contrast
with others whom she regards as 'dull' but her model of
the 'bright' and the 'dull' child will not be at all well
defined.   A second problem arises because all ideal typifications (whether subjective or not) reify the people
they are constructed to typify.   It is common, for example,
to hear teachers say of a pupil, 'Yes, I was surprised by
his results.   He's not an intelligent boy you know.'   Intelligence is here regarded as something that is actually
possessed by the pupil as an entity, presumably inside his
head.   In days gone by it was widely believed that all
such qualities, intelligence, humour, melancholy and so
on, were situated in the brain and could be investigated
by an examination of external 'bumps' on the cranium.   As
a habit of mind the spirit of phrenology lingers on long
after the discipline has perished.   Once it is really
understood that intelligence, liveliness, sociability,
emotional maturity and so on, are only descriptive terms
referring to human action, and are not actual qualities

possessed by the mind, the dangers of treating people in a
particular way because of their 'intelligence', or whatever, are greatly reduced.

Psychologists, with the concept of IQ, have more than
any other group been responsible for keeping alive the
notion of mental qualities. An IQ is not a fixed innate
quality somehow possessed by an individual in much the
same way as he might possess brown eyes or curly hair. It
is derived from his performance on a test designed to
correlate with scholastic attainment. All we know from an
IQ is that most people who made similar scores attained a
certain level of educational success. It does not tell us
that a person with a certain score will achieve a given
level of attainment, nor that he has the capacity for such
attainment. If we are dealing with a large number of
people, who are more or less similar, in most respects, to
the original group on which the test was standardised,
then we might reasonably assume that the same general relationship between **scores** and attainment will hold true.
But for any specific individual we have no way of knowing
whether it will hold true or not unless we make it come
true by acting as if it were already true.

An observational study by Rist (1970) provides a sober-
ing account of how teachers come to think of children as
being of a certain kind. Rist wanted to study the processes whereby the teachers' expectations and social interactions give rise to the social organisation of the
class. For nearly three years Rist visited a nursery
school twice a week for sessions of an hour or so. The
school was situated in a 'blighted urban area' and both
teachers and pupils were black. Only eight days after the
children had entered school for the first time the kindergarten teacher assigned children to streamed work groups
which were to survive almost unchanged for the next three
years. Initially, the teacher had no information on the
children which related to their academic performance or
potential. The children's record cards did contain social
information about family structure, medical care, number
of siblings, parents' occupation, possession of a phone
and so on. This, and the teacher's own estimation of external signs, standards of dress, cleanliness, appearance,
social manners, dialect and such like, were sufficient, in
the teacher's view, to allow her to stream by ability.
Rist observed that (p.419):

> Within a few days only a certain group of children were
> continually being called on to lead the class in the
> Pledge of Allegiance, read the weather calendar each
> day, come to the front for 'show and tell' periods,
> take messages to the office, count the number of child-

ren present in the class, pass out materials for class
projects, be in charge of equipment on the playground,
and lead the class to the bathroom, library or on a
school tour.
Each group was allocated a reading book - individual reading was not encouraged - and so there was no way a child
could demonstrate his ability to cope with a higher graded
text.

This division of the class into those expected to learn
and those not expected to learn was, of course, understood
by the pupils themselves. Those given high status by the
teacher were critical towards those of low status and the
low status children expressed antagonism towards each
other. At the end of the kindergarten year the children
were given a reading test and the scores entered on the
record cards. Considering the teacher's reading policy it
is not in the least surprising to find that the scores re-
flected the initial streaming almost exactly. The first
grade teacher now used these 'objective' scores as the
basis for her grouping. And this process continued right
through to the third year.

This is a particularly vivid example of how teachers
form an 'ideal type' of what is necessary for success,
allow subjective evaluations based on this to influence
their educational judgment, and regard the results of
'objective' tests as somehow independent of their actions,
indeed, as a justification for them. Rist argues that
three alternative explanations might be offered for his
observations. First, that the differential treatment the
children received from their teachers may have affected
their attainment. Second, that the pre-school knowledge
and experience of middle-class children made them better
able to cope with the demands of these teachers. Third,
that some children did, in fact, possess better academic
potential than others and that the teachers were intuit-
ively able to discern these differences. The third alternative, as Rist notes, is that least susceptible to
empirical verification.

Infant classes structured so rigidly as these are uncommon in Britain. It is particularly unlikely that a
British teacher would forbid individual reading. Streaming by table, however, is a quite normal practice and
almost certainly has the same harmful effects. Classroom
organisation and its influence on patterns of teacher-
pupil interaction is the other major theme of direct interest to those who work in the schools. No one supposes
that teachers should attempt to give exactly equal amounts
of attention to all children in her class or that she
should distribute her praise and blame equitably. Some

children will need more attention than others and some
will deserve more blame than praise. What research shows,
however, is that it seems to be the brighter children who
get the most attention - the reverse of what teachers generally believe should be and is happening.

PATTERNS OF INTERACTION

The fullest research into the effects of classroom structure on interaction patterns has been carried out by Adams
and Biddle (1970). These researchers used video-camera to
record the 'real life behaviour of teachers and pupils in
their natural habitat'. In the initial study sixteen
primary and secondary school classrooms were observed for
some two hours each. The classrooms were situated in
middle-class schools with a 'positive, progressive' approach. Analysis of the tapes revealed an 'action zone'
which focused on the centre front and extended directly
from that point to about the middle of the room. It is
within this 'action zone' covering less than a quarter of
the floor space that most of the teacher-pupil interactions went on. Nearly three-quarters of all teacher questions were directed to children located in this space and
more than two-thirds of all pupil-initiated discussion
came from children in this space. The teacher was phys-
ically within this area for more than two-thirds of the
time. She spent 15 per cent of the time walking about the
rest of the room and was either visiting specific locat-
ions or out of the room during the remainder of the time.
Unfortunately Adams and Biddle's research is ridden with
an impossible jargon (they refer to 'emitters', 'targets'
and 'public communicatory systems' and so on) but there is
little doubt of the importance of their general finding:
that participation in lessons is dominated to an extraordinary degree by physical location. Children who sit at
the sides or back of the room play only a very passive
role in the class.
     The researchers assure us that these were 'good'
schools. They do not sound progressive to British ears
but we should not forget that classrooms arranged in this
way, children seated in rows of desks facing the teacher
at the front, are unquestionably the normal type in British secondary schools, and, I suspect, in most junior
schools too. The patterns of interaction which they seem
to create are likely to be most apparent, and have the
most detrimental effects, in oral language work and discussion lessons.
     Unintentionally differential patterns of interaction

can only be altered if the teacher is made aware of them.
The only problem seems to be how this awareness can be
achieved. Merely informing the teacher is inadequate -
the teacher has to realise the implications of what she is
doing and to want to establish wider and more educative
patterns of interaction. Perhaps this is an area where
feedback from video-recordings might be useful. Alter-
natively, two teachers who have a relationship of trust
and respect might find it valuable to observe each other's
lessons and discuss what elements of their approach, if
any, they want to modify.

Self-criticism of this sort is the only criticism that
really works. Yet teachers have modes of thought which
are particularly inimical to the development of a self-
critical analysis of their actions. A stimulating article
by Keddie (1971) demonstrates how teachers involved in
designing and teaching a new integrated curriculum strived
to resolve some of the contradictions which they encount-
ered by maintaining ambiguities of meaning. Giving one
example Keddie writes (p.136):

    a resolution is partially effected by shifting the
    meaning of motivation from an assertion of the desir-
    able in the educationist context to an explanation of
    the desirable in the teacher context. Thus the educa-
    tionist assumes that in the ideal environment of the
    unstreamed school with an undifferentiated curriculum,
    the differential motivation which now leads to under
    achievement will be greatly reduced.... In the teacher
    context, in which the teachers move in their everyday
    activities as teachers motivation becomes an explan-
    ation of pupils' behaviour.

In other, and I hope, more simple words, the meaning of
motivation is shifted from (a) an attitude of pupils which
can be modified by curriculum change and so providing one
of the central reasons for such change to (b) a static
part of the child's personality which explains why he does
not do well even when following the altered curriculum.
In logic one cannot have it both ways; in practice one
does.

    This kind of insight goes a long way towards explaining
why certain children do not do well with the integrated
curriculum - although the teachers have recognised the
educative reasons for modifying the curriculum they still
maintain ideal typifications constructed on the basis of
their experience of children learning within the context
of a non-integrated curriculum. It is an analysis which
could only have been made by an academic researcher working within a fairly well-defined theoretical framework.
Keddie examines the introduction of the new curriculum not

in a traditional way but by a systematic examination of
the classroom situation.

CLASSROOM STUDIES

The interest in classroom based studies indicates the det-
ermination of researchers to get to grips with the ordinary conditions of learning in schools. What seems so
astonishing is that it should have taken so long.   There
are several reasons. First, it is expensive. An observer
who spends a term observing in a classroom must be paid:
ten such observers must be paid ten times as much. And
scale is important in traditional educational research for
the conventional methodologies demand large samples.   A
second drawback has been the teachers' desire to preserve
their privacy and autonomy. In the formal classroom an
observer at the back was all too visible and it was inevitable that most teachers - whose only experience of
people sitting in on their lessons were of headteachers,
HMIs and college tutors - would regard the presence of a
research observer as threatening. Changes in classroom
organisation, especially in primary schools, have made
this much less of a problem. In some informal classrooms
the observer can be relatively unobtrusive, I sometimes
tuck myself actually out of sight in the reading corner!
A further reason inhibiting the development of classroom
research was the assumption that the important educational
determinants were to be found outside the classroom - in
the home for preference. Without being unduly cynical we
can see that teachers can be expected to have a vested
interest in maintaining this assumption. It supports a
particularly crude, but useful, position: of a child who
does well it can be said, 'We taught him successfully.'
and of a child who fails it can be said, 'Terrible background. Can't expect anything else.'
     Perhaps the major drawback to the development of class-
room based research has been the lack of an acceptable
methodology. Fortunately, now that classroom research has
been seen as a plausible enterprise the appropriate techniques are being found; interaction schedules, 'anthropological' descriptions, sound and video recordings, participant observation skills and so on. The studies that have
been carried out so far have demonstrated how these approaches can illuminate classroom reality, and relate the
actions of teachers and pupils to learning processes. And
where a genuine understanding can be created between those
who carry out academic research into classroom learning
and those who work in the schools, there can we expect to
find the most profitable studies.

Suggestions for further reading

GENERAL

Research into perception, expectation and classroom processes deals with an area on the boundaries of social psychology and sociology. It is therefore particularly difficult to refer the reader to other overall surveys. Perhaps one should start with D.H. Hargreaves, 'Interpersonal
Relations in Education' (Routledge & Kegan Paul, 1972) who
discusses these issues from the standpoint of social psychology. And with M.D.F. Young (ed.), 'Knowledge and Control' (Collier-Macmillan, 1971) where several writers
offer a sociological perspective to some related problems.

INTERACTIONIST THEORY

The account given of relevant theory in the initial chapter is based on my interpretation of G.H. Mead and Alfred
Schutz. The interested student will obviously want to
refer to their works. Although they are far from easy to
understand neither writer is voluminous and the books
given in the references are their most important. There
are good accounts of Mead's position in J. Douglas,
'Understanding Everyday Life' (Routledge & Kegan Paul,
1971), J.G. Manise and B.N. Mielzer (eds.), 'Symbolic Interaction' (Allyn & Bacon, 1967) and A.M. Rose, 'Human Behaviour and Processes in Human Interaction' (Routledge &
Kegan Paul, 1962). The recent re-discovery of Schutz is
documented in P. Filmer, M. Phillipson, D. Silverman and
D. Walsh in 'New Directions in Sociological Theory'
(Collier-Macmillan, 1972). Very recently two articles in
the 'British Journal of Sociology' have argued against
Schutz, or at least against what the writers see as a misinterpretation of his position; R.A. Gorman, Alfred

Schutz - an exposition and critique ('British Journal of
Sociology', vol. XXVI, no. 1, pp. 1-19, 1975) and R.E.
Best, New directions in sociological theory: a critical
note on phenomenological sociology and its antecedents
('British Journal of Sociology', vol. XXVI, no. 2, pp.
133-43, 1975). Gorman presents a fair account but crit-
icizes Schutz on the grounds that he is not a Marxist.
Best is concerned to show that certain sociologists who
claim to follow Schutz are, in fact, not doing so.

EXPECTATIONS

The principal study R. Rosenthal and L. Jacobson, 'Pygmalion in the Classroom' (Holt, Rinehart & Winston, 1968)
should certainly be read. Students who are interested in
how acrimonious debates between academics can become are
referred to the 'Journal of Educational Psychology' from
1968 onwards. A considered view is presented by D. Pidgeon, 'Expectation and Pupil Performance' (NFER, 1970).

CLASSROOM ATMOSPHERE

The outstanding work, published too late to be mentioned
in the text, is now E. Wragg, 'Teaching Teaching' (David
& Charles, 1975).

SELF-CONCEPT

The best general account is to be found in D.H. Hargreaves,
'Interpersonal Relations in Education' (Routledge & Kegan
Paul, 1972). There are other works but none are suitable
as an introduction to the field. An exception is J.B.
Thomas, School organisation and self-concept 'Durham
Research Review', vol. VII, no. 33, pp. 929-37).

THE PUPILS' PERSPECTIVE

Very little worthwhile research has been conducted in this
area. Again one has to turn to D.H. Hargreaves, 'Interpersonal Relations in Education' for a good overall view.
A. Morrison and D. McIntyre 'Teachers and Teaching' (Pen-
guin, 1969) also give some useful material. Apart from
these, and my own work mentioned in the references, there
is nothing that can be specially recommended.

NOTE

The Open University run what must be the best education
course available anywhere. Moreover, a good part of it,
in the form of Open University publications and broad-
casts, is available to everyone. They may not need my
recommendation but anyone interested in the issues discussed in this book, and in other aspects of education,
should not neglect the material produced by the Open
University.

Bibliography

ADAMS, R.S. and BIDDLE, B.J. (1970), 'Realities of Teaching: Explorations with Video-Tape', Holt, Rinehart & Winston.
AMIDON, E. and FLANDERS, N.A. (1961), The effects of direct and indirect influences on dependent prone students learning geometry, 'Journal of Educational Psychology', vol. 52, no. 6, pp. 286-91.
AMIDON, E. and SIMON, A. (1965), Teacher-pupil interaction, 'Review of Educational Research', vol. 35, no.2, pp. 130-9.
ANDERSON, H.H. and BREWER, H.M. (1945 and 1946), Studies of teachers' classroom personalities, 'Applied Psychology Monographs', Stanford University Press.
BANNISTER, D. and MAIR, J.M.M. (1968), 'The Evaluation of Personal Constructs', Academic Press.
BARBER, T.X. and SILVER, H.J. (1968), Fact, fiction and the experimenter bias effect, 'Psychological Bulletin', Monograph Supplement, vol. 70, no. 6, part 2, pp. 1-29.
BARKER LUNN, J.C. (1970), 'Streaming in the Primary School', Slough, NFER.
BECKER, H.S. (1952), Social class variations in the teacher-pupil relationship, 'Journal of Educational Sociology', vol. 25, pp. 451-65; reprinted in B.R. Cosin et al. (eds), 'School and Society: a Sociological Reader', Routledge & Kegan Paul with Open University Press, (1972).
BEEZ, W.V. (1968), Influence of biased psychological reports on teacher behaviour and pupil performance, 'Proceedings of the 76th Annual Convention of the American Psychological Association', no. 3, pp. 605-6.
BIDDLE, B.J. and ADAMS, R.S. (1967), 'The Analysis of Classroom Activities', Columbia Press, University of Michigan.
BOARD OF EDUCATION (1938), 'Report of the Consultative Committee on Secondary Education with Special Reference to

Grammar Schools and Technical High Schools', London
(Spens Report).

BOYD, R.D. and DE VAULT, M.V. (1966), The observation and
recording of behaviour, 'Review of Educational Research',
vol. 36, no. 5, pp. 529-49.

BROOKOVER, W.B., LE PERE, J.M., HAMACHEK, D.E., SHAILER,
T. and ERICKSON, E.L. (1965), 'Self-concept of Ability and
School Achievement II', Educational Research Series, no.
31, Bureau of Educational Research Services, College of
Education, University of Michigan.

BROOKOVER, W.B., ERICKSON, E.L. and JONES, L.M. (1967),
'Self-concept of Ability and School Achievement III',
Educational Publishing Services, College of Education,
University of Michigan.

BURSTALL, C. (1968), French in the primary school: some
early findings, 'Journal of Curriculum Studies', vol. 2,
no. 1, pp. 48-58.

BUTCHER, H.J. (ed.) (1968), 'Educational Research in Britain', University of London Press.

CENTRAL ADVISORY COUNCIL FOR EDUCATION (ENGLAND) (1963),
'Half our Future', London (Newsom Report).

CENTRAL ADVISORY COUNCIL FOR EDUCATION (ENGLAND) (1967),
'Children and their Primary Schools', London (Plowden
Report).

CLAIBORN, W.L. (1969), Expectancy effects in the classroom; a failure to replicate, 'Journal of Educational
Psychology', vol. 60, pp. 377-83.

DAVIDSON, H.H. and LANG, G. (1960), Children's perceptions
of their teachers' feelings toward them related to self-
perception, school achievement and behaviour, 'Journal of
Experimental Education', vol. 29, no. 2, pp. 107-18.

DOUGLAS, J.W.B. (1964), 'The Home and the School', Mac-
Gibbon & Kee.

DUTHIE, J.H. (1970), 'Primary School Survey', Scottish
Education Department.

FERRI, E. (1971), 'Streaming: Two Years Later', Slough,
NFER.

FLANDERS, N. (1970), 'Analysing Teaching Behaviour',
Addison-Wesley.

FLEMING, E.S. and ANTTONEN, R.G. (1971), Teacher expectancy or my fair lady, 'AERA Journal', vol. 8, pp. 241.

FORD, J. (1969), 'Social Class and the Comprehensive
School', Routledge & Kegan Paul.

FRIEDMAN, N. (1967), 'The Social Nature of Psychological
Research', Basic Books, New York.

GAGE, N.L. (ed.) (1963), 'Handbook of Research on Teaching', Rand McNally.

GARNER, J. and BING, M. (1973), Inequalities of teacher-
pupil contacts, 'British Journal of Educational Psychol-

ogy', vol. 43, no. 5, pp. 234-43.

GOOD, T.L. and BROPHY, J.E. (1970), Teacher-child dyadic interactions: a new method of classroom observation, 'Journal of School Psychology', vol. 8, no. 2, pp. 131-8.

GOOD, T.L. and BROPHY, J.E. (1972), Behavioural expression of teacher attitudes, 'Journal of Educational Psychology', vol. 63, no. 6, pp. 617-24.

GOODACRE, E.J. (1968), 'Teachers and their Pupils' Home Background', Slough, NFER.

HALLWORTH, H.J. (1962), A teacher's perception of his pupils, 'Educational Review', vol. 14, pp. 124-33.

HARGREAVES, D.H. (1967), 'Social Relations in a Secondary School', Routledge & Kegan Paul.

HARGREAVES, D.H. (1972), 'Interpersonal Relations in Education', Routledge & Kegan Paul.

HENRY, J. (1963), 'Culture Against Man', Random House (Tavistock, 1966).

JACKSON, B. (1964), 'Streaming: an Education System in Miniature', Routledge & Kegan Paul.

JACKSON, P.W. (1968), 'Life in Classrooms', Holt, Rinehart & Winston.

JACKSON, P.W. and LAHADERNE, H.M. (1967), 'Inequalities of teacher-pupil contacts', 'Psychology in the Schools', vol. 4, pp. 204-11.

JACKSON, P.W., SILBERMAN, M.L. and WOLFSON, B.J. (1969), Signs of personal involvement in teachers' descriptions of their students, 'Journal of Educational Psychology', vol. 60, no. 1, pp. 22-7.

KEDDIE, N. (1971), Classroom knowledge, in M.D.F. Young, 'Knowledge and Control', Collier-Macmillan.

KELLY, G.A. (1955), 'The Psychology of Personal Constructs', Norton.

LIPPET, R. and WHITE, R.K. (1943), An experimental study of group life, in E.E. MacCoby, T.M. Newcomb and E.L. Hartley, 'Readings in Social Psychology', Methuen, 1968.

MCINTYRE, D., MORRISON, A. and SUTHERLAND, J. (1966), Social and educational variables relating to teachers' assessments of primary school pupils, 'British Journal of Educational Psychology', vol. 36, pp. 272-9.

MEAD, G.H. (1934), 'Mind, Self and Society' (ed. C.W. Morris), University of Chicago Press.

MEDLEY, D.M. and MITZEL, H.E. (1958), A technique for measuring classroom behaviour, 'Journal of Educational Psychology', vol. 49, no. 2, pp. 86-92.

MILGRAM, S. (1965), Some conditions of obedience and disobedience to authority, 'Human Relations', vol. 18, pp. 57-76.

NASH, R. (1973), 'Classrooms Observed', Routledge & Kegan Paul.

NASH, R. (1974), Pupils' expectations for their teachers, 'Research in Education', no. 12, pp. 47-61.

ORNE, M.T. (1962), On the social psychology of the psychological experiment with particular reference to demand characteristics and their implications, 'American Psychology', vol. 17, pp. 776-83.

PALARDY, J.M. (1969), What teachers believe - what children achieve, 'Elementary School Journal', no. 69, pp. 370-4.

PALFREY, C.F. (1973), Headteachers' expectations and their pupils' self-concepts, 'Educational Research', pp. 123-7.

PERKINS, H.V. (1958), Teachers' and peers' perceptions of children's self-concepts, 'Child Development', vol. 29, pp. 203-20.

PIDGEON, D.A. (1970), 'Expectation and pupil performance', Slough, NFER.

RIST, R.C. (1970), Student social class and teacher expectations: the self-fulfilling prophecy in ghetto education, 'Harvard Educational Review', 40, 3. pp. 411-51.

ROSENTHAL, R. and JACOBSON, L. (1968), 'Pygmalion in the Classroom', Holt, Rinehart & Winston.

ROSENTHAL, R. and LAWSON, R. (1964), A longitudinal study of the effects of experimenter bias on the operant learning of a laboratory rat, 'Journal of Psychiatric Research' vol. 2, pp. 61-72.

ROTHBART, M., DALFEN, S. and BARRETT, R. (1971), Effects of teachers' expectancy on student-teacher interaction, 'Journal of Educational Psychology', vol. 62, no. 1, pp. 49-54.

RUBOVITS, P.C. and MAEHR, M.L. (1973), Pygmalion black and white, 'Journal of Personality and Social Psychology', vol. 25, no. 2, pp. 210-18.

SCHULTZ, D.P. (1969), The human subject in psychological science, 'Psychological Bulletin', vol. 72, no. 3, pp. 214-28.

SCHUTZ, A. (1932/67), 'The Phenomenology of the Social World', translated by G. Walsh, Northwestern University Press.

SILBERMAN, M.L. (1969), Behavioural expression of teachers' attitudes towards elementary school students, 'Journal of Educational Psychology'. vol. 60, no. 5, pp. 402-7.

SNOW, R. (1969), Review of 'Pygmalion in the Classroom' by Rosenthal and Jacobson, 'Contemporary Psychology', vol. 14, no. 4, pp. 708-11.

TAYLOR, P.H. (1962), Children's evaluations of the characteristics of the good teacher, 'British Journal of Educational Psychology', vol. 32, pp. 258-66.

THORNDIKE, R.L. (1968), Review of 'Pygmalion in the

Classroom' by Rosenthal and Jacobson, 'AERA Journal', vol.
5, no. 4, p. 708.
WEBER, M. (1922/64), 'The Theory of Social and Economic
Organisation', translated by A.M. Henderson and T. Parsons
(ed. T. Parsons), Oxford University Press.
WESTBURY, I. and BELLACK, A. (1971), 'Research into Class-
room Processes: Recent Developments and Next Steps'.
Teachers College Press, New York.
WITHALL, J. (1951), The development of the Climate Index,
'Journal of Educational Research', vol. 45, pp. 93-100.
WYLIE, R. (1961), 'The Self Concept', University of Neb-
raska Press.